PUBLIC SCANDALS:
Sexual Orientation and Criminal Law in Romania

A report by Human Rights Watch and the International Gay and Lesbian Human Rights Commission

New York · Washington · London · Brussels

Printed in the United States of America

ISBN 1-56432-178-9
Library of Congress Catalog Card Number: 98-84053

Human Rights Watch is dedicated to
protecting the human rights of people around the world.

We stand with victims and activists to prevent
discrimination, to uphold political freedom, to protect people from
inhumane conduct in wartime, and to bring offenders to justice.

We investigate and expose
human rights violations and hold abusers accountable.

We challenge governments and those who hold power to end
abusive practices and respect international human rights law.

We enlist the public and the international
community to support the cause of human rights for all.

HUMAN RIGHTS WATCH

Human Rights Watch conducts regular, systematic investigations of human rights abuses in some seventy countries around the world. Our reputation for timely, reliable disclosures has made us an essential source of information for those concerned with human rights. We address the human rights practices of governments of all political stripes, of all geopolitical alignments, and of all ethnic and religious persuasions. Human Rights Watch defends freedom of thought and expression, due process and equal protection of the law, and a vigorous civil society; we document and denounce murders, disappearances, torture, arbitrary imprisonment, discrimination, and other abuses of internationally recognized human rights. Our goal is to hold governments accountable if they transgress the rights of their people.

Human Rights Watch began in 1978 with the founding of its Europe and Central Asia division (then known as Helsinki Watch). Today, it also includes divisions covering Africa, the Americas, Asia, and the Middle East. In addition, it includes three thematic divisions on arms, children's rights, and women's rights. It maintains offices in New York, Washington, Los Angeles, London, Brussels, Moscow, Dushanbe, Rio de Janeiro, and Hong Kong. Human Rights Watch is an independent, nongovernmental organization, supported by contributions from private individuals and foundations worldwide. It accepts no government funds, directly or indirectly.

Addresses for Human Rights Watch
350 Fifth Avenue, 34th Floor, New York, NY 10118-3299
Tel: (212) 290-4700, Fax: (212) 736-1300, E-mail: hrwnyc@hrw.org

1522 K Street, N.W., #910, Washington, DC 20005-1202
Tel: (202) 371-6592, Fax: (202) 371-0124, E-mail: hrwdc@hrw.org

33 Islington High Street, N1 9LH London, UK
Tel: (171) 713-1995, Fax: (171) 713-1800, E-mail: hrwatchuk@gn.apc.org

15 Rue Van Campenhout, 1000 Brussels, Belgium
Tel: (2) 732-2009, Fax: (2) 732-0471, E-mail: hrwatcheu@gn.apc.org

Web Site Address: http://www.hrw.org
Listserv address: To subscribe to the list, send an e-mail message to majordomo@igc.apc.org with "subscribe Human Rights Watch-news" in the body of the message (leave the subject line blank).

***

Addresses for the International Gay and Lesbian Human Rights Commission

Main Office:
IGLHRC
1360 Mission Street, Suite 200
San Francisco, CA 94103, USA
Tel: +1-415-255-8680, Fax: +1-415-255-8662

New York Office:
IGLHRC
c/o Human Rights Watch
350 Fifth Avenue, 34th Floor
New York, NY 10018-3299, USA
Tel: +1-212-216-1814, Fax: +1-212-736-1300

Email: iglhrc@iglhrc.org
Website: http://www.iglhrc.org
Listserv address: To receive the Emergency Response Network via email, write to macjordomo@iglhrc.org (*not* majordomo) with the following message:
For the English version: "subscribe ern-en <your first name> <your last name>".
For the Spanish version: "subscribe ern-es <your first name> <your last name>".
For the French version: "subscribe ern-fr <your first name> <your last name>".

The International Gay and Lesbian Human Rights Commission (IGLHRC) protects and advances the fundamental human rights of lesbians, gay men, bisexuals, transgendered people, people living with HIV or AIDS, and other sexual minorities throughout the world. IGLHRC responds to human rights violations on the basis of sexual orientation, gender identity, and HIV sero-status through documentation, advocacy, coalition building, public education, technical assistance, and internal development. In addition to working in coalition with local and national sexual minority groups in countries around the world, IGLHRC both advocates and cooperates with inter-governmental bodies and human rights organizations, as well as other social movement organizations. IGLHRC advocates not only for the human rights concerns of local constituencies, but for human rights as a framework that local constituencies can themselves employ.

International Gay and Lesbian Human Rights Commission (IGLHRC)

Established in 1990 as a U.S.-based non-profit non-governmental organization, IGLHRC responds to human rights violations on the basis of sexual orientation, gender identity, and HIV sero-status through documentation, advocacy, coalition building, public education, technical assistance, and internal development.

IGLHRC documents the persecution, resistance, and activism of lesbians, gays, bisexuals, transvestites, transsexuals, and people with HIV or AIDS around the globe. This documentation bolsters our advocacy for political, legal, and social change. IGLHRC works at local, national, regional, and international levels to change public policy and mobilize effective action in defense of human rights, through our Emergency Response Network, our Asylum Project, and other special projects and campaigns.

In the struggle to expand the human rights of sexual minorities, IGLHRC partners with grassroots organizations all over the world, as well as with U.S.-based lesbian, gay, bisexual and transgendered groups and international human rights organizations. IGLHRC is committed to defending and preserving the self-determination of the local groups and individuals with whom we cooperate. We do not impose a single mold of sexual identity, linguistic terminology, or political action on the multiplicity of forms of sexual practices and identifications around the world. Instead, IGLHRC defends the rights of individuals worldwide to define their own sexualities in their own terms, and to design their political programs on that basis.

Our staff members are Dusty Aráujo, Asylum Project Coordinator; Jennifer Carson, Information Specialist; Julie Dorf, Executive Director; Scott Long, Advocacy Coordinator and Regional Specialist—Europe; Huy (Rolland) Le, Administrative Assistant; Sydney Levy, Program Director; Michael Mills, Office Manager; Leslie Minot, Development Associate; Mirka Negroni, Regional Specialist—Latin America, United States and Canada; Mary Sigaji, Regional Specialist—Africa, Middle East and the Caribbean.

The members of the board of directors are Ron Buckmire, Nan Buzard, Alexandra Chasin, Joe Collins, Marcia de Castro, Julie Dorf, Gerard Fergerson, Katherine Franke, Emily Honig, Tinku Ali Ishtiaq, Gara LaMarche, Chun Liu, Julie Mertus, Vinh-Kim Nguyen, Jairo Enrique Pedraza, Darius Rejali, and Stephanie Roth.

CONTENTS

1. SUMMARY AND RECOMMENDATIONS

> I was nineteen and this was the most terrible thing that had happened in my life. I understood that I was a criminal; and I saw, too, that my only crime was myself. I hated myself; I hated this country, too, because I suddenly saw that it hated me and it had always hated me . . . As I sat in my cell and the terror of the days increased, my hair began to turn grey.
>
> *--Florin Hopris, 19, Sibiu, May 1993*

> Sometimes on the street I pass one of the policemen who beat me that night, and I remember how they called me a cocksucker and a pervert, how they laughed at me, how they stuck my head down the toilet . . . I wish there were someone to punish them for the way they punished me. Instead I am afraid to look at them. I look away.
>
> *--Radu Vasiliu, 18, Iasi, June 1997*

Today in Romania, gays and lesbians are routinely denied some of the most basic human rights guaranteed by international law. Despite amendments in 1996 to the criminal code provisions relating to homosexual conduct—portrayed by the Romanian government as a total repeal of legislation criminalizing consensual sexual relations between adults of the same sex—gays and lesbians continue to be arrested and convicted for such relations if they become public knowledge. Moreover, they face frequent physical abuse and harassment by law enforcement officials, as well as systematic discrimination in many walks of life. Romanian law not only prohibits private sexual acts between consenting adults of the same sex, but may also be interpreted to punish speech and association that expresses a homosexual identity—or even support of such identity.

For decades in Romania, all consensual sexual relations between adults of the same sex were forbidden. Numerous legal provisions created the framework for the criminalization of homosexual conduct, for legally-tolerated discrimination, and for denying gays and lesbians the equal protection of the law. Most significantly, Article 200, paragraph 1, of the 1968 Romanian criminal code stated: "Sexual relations between persons of the same sex are punishable by imprisonment of one to five years." Paragraph 2 dealt with homosexual relations with a minor or by force, establishing higher penalties than were the case for heterosexual relations with a minor or heterosexual rape. Finally, paragraph 4 of Article 200 punished "inciting or encouraging a person to practice" the acts described in paragraph 1 with one to five years' imprisonment.

In 1996, after intense debate, and largely as a result of international pressure—especially from the Council of Europe—Article 200, paragraph 1 was amended to punish homosexual acts "committed in public, or if causing public scandal" with one to five years' imprisonment. At the same time, language was also added to the last paragraph, to punish "inciting or encouraging a person to the practice of sexual relations between persons of the same sex, *as well as propaganda* or *association or any other act of proselytism* [italics added]," with the same prison terms. Although the Romanian government presents this language as a liberalization, the expansively worded law ensures that those who engage in consensual sex in private can continue to face prosecution: the acts need only become known to instigate legal reprisal. It is, in fact, their "becoming known" which is now illegal. In contemporary Romania, *being* gay or lesbian—having a public identity as such, and a sexual orientation different from the majority—is, effectively, against the law.

"Sexual orientation" is a term of relatively recent coinage. Yet, describing as it does an intricate complex of factors which determine the objects of one's sexual and emotional desires, it defines a profound and rooted aspect of each individual's personality and humanity. For heterosexuals as well as for lesbians, gay men, bisexuals, and transgendered persons, this part of one's self is a place of needs and desires which are deep, intimate, and interior. For heterosexuals as well as for lesbians, gays, bisexuals, and transgendered persons, however, it also permeates the remainder of one's selfhood in ways both conscious and unconscious, casual and meaningful. It is experienced not just inwardly but through acts, gestures, and expressions, through assertions of similarity or dissimilarity from others, through hands held or touches exchanged, through conversational allusions to a partner, husband, or wife. For heterosexuals as well as for lesbians, gays, bisexuals and transgendered persons, identifying and voicing one's sexual orientation can be as important to the constitution and growth of a self as can one's race, ethnicity, gender, or religious conviction. Like those categories, it can be a significant side of the identity one shows the world. And as with those categories, discrimination or the denial of the equal protection of the law on the basis of sexual orientation violates internationally protected rights.

Article 2 of the International Covenant on Civil and Political Rights (ICCPR) states: "Each State Party to the present Covenant undertakes to respect and to ensure to all individuals within its territory and subject to its jurisdiction the rights recognized in the present Covenant, without distinction of any kind, such as race, color, sex, language, religion, political or other opinion, national or social origin, birth or other status. In a 1994 decision against a law similar to Article 200, the United Nations Human Rights Committee held that sexual orientation is not a valid basis for according discriminatory enjoyment of rights specified in the ICCPR.

Article 200 of the Romanian penal code on its face violates this human rights norm, in that it punishes conduct between persons of the same sex that, when carried on by persons of opposite sexes, is either not criminal or receives a lower penalty. Even its criminalization of sexual acts "committed in public" is discriminatory: no comparable provision of the penal code punishes, or even mentions, heterosexual sexual acts committed in public.

The violation of one right in particular has occasioned the most widespread condemnation of "sodomy laws." Both the ICCPR (Article 17) and the European Convention for the Protection of Human Rights and Fundamental Freedoms (Article 8) guarantee the right to privacy. In three successive decisions, the European Court of Human Rights has held that such "sodomy laws" contravene the European Convention's privacy protections. Article 200, along with similar laws which remain in force in numerous jurisdictions worldwide, violates this right in making consensual, private sexual behavior between adults subject to prosecution.

Yet the most invidious effect of these laws transcends their simple denial of privacy. They codify discrimination against a class of persons on the basis of an intrinsic aspect of their personality and humanity. They punish and persecute those unwilling to suppress all evidence of that central characteristic. Similar in this way to policies of assimilation forced upon ethnic minorities, or compulsory conversions imposed upon religious believers, they require individuals to eradicate a part of—a possibility inherent in—their deepest selves.

The implications of Article 200 thus go beyond what a legislator, at its first promulgation in 1936, called "the secrecy of rooms." Both the past history of the law, and its present status, reveal its goal as ensuring that an extensive range of rights will be denied to gays and lesbians. The law enforces inequality: it dictates that behaviors and expressions which identify people as gay or lesbian—whether they be sexual acts behind closed doors, or casual gestures of intimacy on the street—will be stripped of protection.

In researching this report, Human Rights Watch and the International Gay and Lesbian Human Rights Commission have discovered that arrests continue under the new version of Article 200, enabled by the failure of the legislators who wrote the law, as well as of local prosecutors and police, to define what the new language means. Equally important, however, the continued existence of Article 200—as well as of other repressive or simply vague legal provisions which can be invoked against a despised minority—contributes to a climate of legalized intolerance. Officials, whether in police stations, prisons, courtrooms, or hospitals, are routinely encouraged to regard gays and lesbians as persons without rights. Once arrested, those accused of violating Article 200 are routinely beaten by police, and while in detention are targeted by other inmates for sexual abuse, with the tolerance and even encouragement of guards. Throughout Romania, meeting places of lesbians and gays, as well as the few organizations that have attempted to form, exist, if at all, under the continual threat of legal harassment. And it is widely accepted that a legitimate national purpose is served by eradicating homosexuality completely from public view.

These phenomena are not just recent ones. From their first criminalization in 1936, homosexual *acts* were punished in Romania lest they give rise to homosexual *identity* and *community*. The law aimed to eliminate that identity and that community, seen as foreign, inauthentic, and contagious, from the national life. Private acts were penalized preemptively, before they could become public and infect a putatively sterilized public sphere. As a legislator opposed to any tolerance of homosexuality argued in 1995:

> What is repellent and immoral in the street cannot be either moral or permitted in intimacy. Such a solution is contradictory, hypocritical. By nature, such acts will then be encouraged to transgress from the interior to the exterior, this being only the start of an aberrant behavior which will become more and more aggressive and, in the end, impossible to combat.

From this perspective, any homosexual act is potentially exposed and open, essentially "propaganda" to be silenced. Prohibiting expression and association, preventing homosexuals from speaking or showing themselves in the ordinary gestures others enjoy and employ daily, were purposes of the law from the very beginning.

Article 200 in its various forms tries to impose a silence so complete that the acts it penalizes cannot even be unequivocally named. In so doing, it legitimates unequal enjoyment of basic human rights—to expression, association, assembly—by which emotion and experience are shared. Its survival measures the incompleteness of democratization in Romania. It betrays a refusal to allow unfettered voice and visibility to all.

The legal status of gays and lesbians—their ability to move and appear in public, to speak out and act together—is a test of the civic openness without which a civil society cannot be constructed or sustained. Gays and lesbians lay claim to equal rights. That such a claim constitutes "public scandal" reveals the boundaries of democracy in Romania today.

Summary Recommendations

Human Rights Watch and the International Gay and Lesbian Human Rights Commission therefore call on the government of Romania:

- to bring an end to beatings, maltreatment, and other forms of abuse practiced by police and other officials on the basis of victims' perceived sexual orientation, and to punish those found responsible for such abuses in the past.

- to eliminate all laws which permit, encourage, or enforce discrimination against persons based on their perceived sexual orientation. These include not only Article 200 of the Romanian penal code, but also a series of other laws by which gays and lesbians are prosecuted and/or more severely penalized than heterosexuals who engage in similar acts;

- to eliminate all laws which can be used to punish individuals for consensual, private homosexual acts between adults;

- to clarify or repeal ambiguous legal provisions which can be used to persecute individuals for peacefully exercising rights of expression, association, and assembly, as well as laws that arbitrarily interfere with privacy;

Human Rights Watch and the International Gay and Lesbian Human Rights Commission call on international bodies, including the Council of Europe, the Organization for Security and Cooperation in Europe, and the European Union:

- to press the government of Romania to undertake the above reforms;

- to investigate the multiple forms of discrimination based on sexual orientation—in addition to the simple existence or absence of laws explicitly criminalizing homosexual acts—in evaluating the human rights records of applicant as well as member states;

- to investigate and address discrimination based on sexual orientation through their existing mechanisms for rights protection, including mechanisms to protect the rights of minorities.

A detailed description of legal and policy changes needed to enact these recommendations can be found at the end of this report.

2. BACKGROUND

The 1936 Penal Code

In 1936, the parliament of the Kingdom of Romania sat down to talk about sex, in more detail than ever before. The country's penal code, dating from 1864, was being revised;[1] in the process, sexual crimes became a particular focus of dispute. Legislators found themselves engaged not only in condemning, but in recategorizing, a range of sexual acts.

Title 11 of the new code divided sexual offenses into two subcategories. "Infractions against decency" (Articles 419-428) included rape, seduction, and pedophilia. "Infractions against good morals" were more elastic: if these crimes were not uniformly victimless, the identity of particular victims at least faded to insignificance against the offense to a more amorphous public. For all these acts were either performed in or in some way repellent to the public sphere—a sphere implicitly defined by the dissemination of information or the exchange of money. "Traffic in obscene publications," as well as obscene gestures, abused the first function; "incitement to prostitution," procuring, and trafficking in women, all offended the second. *Identifying* certain sexual behaviors, and *delineating* what the public sphere contained, moved hand in hand.

"Infractions against good morals" included a new provision. Article 431 penalized "acts of sexual inversion committed between men or between women, if provoking public scandal," with six months' to two years' imprisonment. From the beginning, the language of this article raised questions. Most of those questions persist in Romania today.

One basic uncertainty was exactly what was being criminalized. Observers today might assume the acts involved were synonymous with "homosexuality." In fact matters were more intricate. Provisions ancestral to the new law referred to "acts of unnatural indecency" or to "indecency against nature, either a) with animals, or b) with persons of the same sex."[2] These injunctions resembled European laws dating from the Middle Ages, which lumped same-sex relations with

---

[1] *Codul Penal 1 Maiu 1865 cu modificarile din 1874, 1882, 1893, 1894, 1895—Textul Codului Penal si Procedurii Penale.* Editura Libraria Noua, Bucuresti, 1908. See also HOSI Wien/Auslandsgruppe, *Rosa Liebe unter dem Roten Stern. Zur Lage der Lesben und Schwulen in Osteuropa,* Fruhlings Erwachen Verlag, Hamburg, 1984, pp. 42-43.

[2] Transilvania, Art. 242; Bucovina, § 129 (both laws from regions annexed to Romania after the war). Ratescu et. al, eds., p. 681. The 1864 code, modeled on the Code Napoleon, had no comparable provision.

other reviled deeds, including bestiality, incest, or non-vaginal heterosexual intercourse, under broad rubrics such as "sodomy" or "unnatural acts."

The legislators wanted more exactitude: but they were quickly mired in lexicographical quagmires. "Homosexuality" was in fact used in the first proposed version of the article. The term was of recent, and foreign, coinage[3], though; some parliamentarians doubted its meaning. It was dropped "because it does not include inverted relations between women."[4]

However, other legal commentators saw "homosexuality" as including lesbian relations—but as different from "pederasty," which "can also be committed between a man and a woman, when the woman is the passive agent (*coitus per anum*)." All these were forms of "sexual inversion," meaning that Article 431 might criminalize *heterosexual* acts as well:

> One might put the question whether a husband who has been mastered by this vice [pederasty], and has exercised the act through violence on his wife, can be found guilty of the act of sexual inversion—sexual relations between husband and wife being obligatory. Doctrine in general agrees that the husband does not have this right and is guilty of the offense of inversion.[5]

These terminological quandaries had a significance beyond the dictionary. The penal code attempted to classify sexual behaviors, so that (for instance) "sexual inversion" could be understood to include "homosexuality" and "pederasty," while

---

[3] It had been coined in 1867 by an Austro-Hungarian doctor, Karoly Kertbeny (or Benkert).

[4] Ratescu et. al, eds., p.680.

[5] Ratescu et. al, eds., p. 681. It is clear, at least, that here "pederasty" is used to refer to anal intercourse *between adults*. (However, the commentary seems to propose a distinction between "pederasty" and "sexual relations" proper. By contrast, in contemporary Romanian legal practice, anal sex is regarded as a *raport sexual* or *relatia sexuala*; oral sex, though, is often instead categorized as mere *perversiune sexuala*. See below, note 99.) The commentator in question was I. Ionescu-Dolj, President of the Legislative Council's Section of Public Law.

bestiality fell into a different column.[6] Legislators were, in fact, inventing "sexualities"—an intellectual labor which had been going on in Western Europe for some time. Sexual acts previously conflated were differentiated, described, placed in categories. Those behaviors were then used to define the identities of (and sometimes to segregate legally and medically) individuals and groups who engaged in them.[7]

The same process by which the category of "homosexual" had been invented in Western Europe was recapitulated in Romania. While in Vienna and Paris the work of physicians and scientists largely drove the process, however, in Bucharest those discourses were silent.[8] The work of classifying sexualities was handed over to the law.

This vacuum of supporting discourse created confusion. There was no clear sense of what "sexual inversion" was: commentators could still invoke "pederasty," "sapphism," and "tribadism," assigning meanings to them almost at will. One closed his notes by falling back on an ancient term (and penalty), almost with relief: "In the old law, sodomites were punished with mutilation and recidivists with burning at the stake."[9]

---

[6] In fact the new code placed "sexual acts committed between humans and animals" in a separate article, 432, and punished them with 3 months' to one year's imprisonment "if provoking public scandal."

[7] Thus Michel Foucault observes "the appearance in nineteenth-century psychiatry, jurisprudence, and literature of a whole series of discourses on the species and subspecies of homosexuality, inversion, pederasty, and 'psychic hermaphroditism'; see Michel Foucault, *The History of Sexuality, Volume I: An Introduction,* trans. R. Hurley, Vintage (New York, 1980), p. 101.

[8] Dr. Valerian Tuculescu, former president of the Association of Free Psychiatrists, remarked to Human Rights Watch and IGLHRC: "Sexuality has never been regarded primarily through the prism of medical knowledge in Romania. It has always been treated as a political and moral problem." Interview by Scott Long and Bogdan Voicu, June 1997.

[9] Ratescu, et. al., eds., p. 681. Partial redundancies in the code as enacted also suggest a breakdown of classifications. For instance, rape is defined in Article 419 as a man forcing "a person of either sex" to enter "a sexual relation"; Article 420 then penalizes for "violence against decency" any person who "commits any act of sexual inversion" by force on another person, imposing a virtually identical penalty but leaving such an act (and its exact distinction from rape) undefined. Apparently "inversion," once again, was something different from a full "sexual relation."

If reticence and privacy prevented a full description of the incriminated acts, there was further uncertainty about *when* they were incriminated. One legislator pleaded: "Do not make this offense depend on provoking public scandal! . . . What interests us is the proven offense, and the prosecutor should prove the offense by any means."[10] The authors who included the "public scandal" language, though, defended it as limiting state power. The committee presenting the text to the two chambers observed, "The law cannot go further in its rigor, penetrating with transparent beams the secrecy of rooms where two accused persons may meet."[11]

Yet questions persisted about how far "public scandal" impinged on either the citizen's body or the "secrecy of rooms." Could private acts become a provocation? A court decision of 1940 suggested that in becoming known at all, "sexual inversion" automatically became culpable: "Acts of sexual inversion fall under the provisions of Article 431 if knowledge about the act is divulged, *as in such a case they provoke public scandal.*"[12] A 1948 commentary agreed:

> . . . the element of "public scandal" is not a purely objective condition of punishability. Rather this element must follow from the

---

[10] Ratescu, et. al, eds., p. 681.

[11] Ratescu, et. al., eds., p. 681.

[12] Cas. II, dec. 297, 1940; cited in V. Papadopol, I. Stoenescu, and G.V. Protopopescu, eds., *Codul Penal al Republicii Populare Romane Adnotat,* Editura de Stat, Bucuresti, 1948, p. 462; emphasis added. This raises the question of whether police or prosecutors could create, then certify, scandal simply by releasing information to the public—a question that would reappear in at least one case from 1990s Romania (sentinta penala 02.03.1993, cazul Radu Alexandru, Tribunal Militar, Bucuresti; discussed in part 5 below) Other jurisprudence cited by the 1948 commentary, however, drew a much narrower circle of admissibility: "The element of provoking public scandal does not exist when this scandal follows from the act of other persons, who through their maneuvers have managed to discover the relations between the accused, and have given them notoriety. The same applies when the authorities have discovered such relations and have made an act of which the public previously knew nothing into a matter for discussion." Papadopol, et. al, p. 462. However, the 1939 commentary strongly implies a broader latitude, citing in lieu of a definition of "scandal" the example of "the well-known public scandal provoked in Germany in 1908, through the revelations of M. Harden against the pederasts, who were discovered as well among official persons." In that case—which outraged Wilhelmine society in its waning days—relations conducted in private among a circle of powerful (and adult) aristocrats indeed became known solely through the broadsides and "maneuvers" of Harden, a crusading journalist.

> manner in which the persons between whom these relations took place comported themselves: namely, that they provoked public scandal through their attitude, either by betraying themselves in a positive act of ostentatious depravity, *or by engaging in a negative act of imprudence and negligence in [not] taking measures necessary to conceal these relations.*[13]

Even if "provoking scandal" necessarily entailed public behavior, its perimeters were still wide. Asked to clarify the term during debate, the text's authors replied, "For example, many persons may be accustomed to meeting in a certain place, and, because the entire world knows that they assemble there, a disturbance of public peace is produced in the vicinity." A 1939 commentator elaborated:

> Scandal is public when the actors, looking to win or to search for clients, no longer make a secret of their relations, and in publicizing the disgusting vice the general moral sentiment is assaulted and public opinion is with good cause alarmed. [14]

Clearly *association* and *expression* were targeted by the language from the first. Indeed, the reference to "clients" in these comments, and the invocation of pornography as a cause of same-sex attraction, strike notes which would reverberate for many years in both legal discourse and the popular imagination in Romania. Inversion merited suppression less as individual vice than as the characteristic of an emergent group. "Sexual inversion" and its constituent behaviors were analogized to prostitution, conceived of as less relation than transaction, and stigmatized as a mode of togetherness impermissible in the public sphere.

Advent of Article 200

The 1936 debates raised lasting issues. They show legislators grappling to delineate both privacy and the public sphere. And this attempt moves in uneasy but inextricable tandem with the effort not just to control but to define sexuality—to make sexual behavior intelligible in juridical terms.

"Sexual inversion" lay in an intermediate zone on the boundaries of intimacy. It was sufficiently private to seem unfamiliar, even indescribable, to most of the

---

[13] Papadopol, et. al., eds., p. 462; emphasis added.

[14] Both in Ratescu, et. al., eds., p. 680.

legislators. Yet even when it took place behind closed doors, it was not defended by the near-absolute immunity which enshrouded the family.[15] Instead it was always on the verge of becoming a public concern. "Sexual inversion" was a site where the limits of private and public were contested.

The 1936 code was an attempt to maintain and extend the half-fact, half-fiction of the rule of law in a country already shaken by a fascist insurgency, government corruption, and endemic abuse of power. The uncertain limits it drew around the state's legitimate zone of control were part of this attempt; but the boundaries it tried to sketch between the "secrecy of rooms" and the public square would soon be even less intelligible. Within two years, King Carol II set up a royal dictatorship. Over the next five decades of first fascist and then communist rule, legal and social protections for privacy and the public sphere would disappear completely.

The 1936 code was not fully revised until 1968, when the Grand National Assembly of what was now the Socialist Republic of Romania adopted a new version. This code embodied not only the realities of a socialist regime in place since the Second World War, but also the shifting intentions of Nicolae Ceausescu after his first three years in power. After a brief liberalization, the regime was beginning to restrict renascent freedoms and resharpen its instruments of control.

The code revised and recategorized all laws on sexuality. A chapter on "infractions involving sexual life" fell within a larger section on "infractions against the person." Three new crimes were specified. Article 202 dealt with "sexual corruption" of a minor (defined as performing "acts of an obscene character" on the minor or in the minor's presence). Article 201, based closely on the former Article 431, punished "acts of sexual perversion which cause public scandal" with one to five years' imprisonment. The article defined sexual perversion as "any unnatural act in connection with sexual life, other than those provided in Article 200." Finally, the first paragraph of the new Article 200 read, "Sexual relations between persons of the same sex are punishable by imprisonment of one to five years."[16]

---

[15] Clearly the heterosexual family lay at the center of what legal concept of "privacy" existed (and the word itself is problematic to translate into in Romanian); the only sexual offenses punishable within the family's penumbra were those which assaulted its sanctity, including adultery, bigamy, and incest. These fell into a title separate from other sexual offenses, as "crimes against the family." Marital rape was explicitly exempted from punishment.

[16] *Codul Penal si Codul de Procedura Penala.* Editura "Cutuma," Bucuresti, 1992. For full texts, see Appendix 1.

Thus, reference to "public scandal" was dropped, and the penalty drastically increased. In a sense, in 1968, "homosexuality" came into existence in Romania, specifically recognized by the law: but only to be banned completely. If the 1936 language drew restrictions around the public sphere, the 1968 code seemed intended to abolish the private. It paralleled Ceausescu's pro-natalist decrees—which compelled women to undergo periodic and compulsory gynecological examinations and severely punished abortions—as a draconian restriction of bodily freedom and an excuse to invade the intimate realm.[17] Yet there is every reason to think that Ceausescu also saw sexual deviance not just as a personal anomaly to be extirpated, but in political terms. To a regime which predicated its authority on its surveillance of every detail of existence, *any* privacy immune to social supervision was a threat.[18]

Article 200 was diplomatically useful to the Ceausescu regime as, with the advent of the 1970s, it tightened virtually every screw of social control. Since Amnesty International and other organizations did not yet recognize persons imprisoned solely for their homosexuality as prisoners of conscience, the dubious and disloyal could be charged under Article 200 without attracting international attention—allowing Ceausescu's human-rights record to remain cosmetically clear. "People who were politically difficult, from 1980 on, were always arrested for theft of public property, for abuses of authority, or for other trumped-up charges—including homosexuality," one politician remembers.[19]

---

[17] Comments by conservative Romanian politicians in the 1990s, which portray homosexuality as an assault on Romanian reproduction, raise the possibility that Ceausescu may have conceived Article 200 at least partly in the context of his own pro-natalist policies designed to raise the birth rate.

[18] Similarly. in justifying a sodomy law introduced in the USSR in 1934, Stalin's chief prosecutor described homosexuality not as a vice but as a political grouping outside state control: "So who are the bulk of our clients in these sorts of cases? Is it the working class? No! It is classless hoodlums . . . either from the dregs of society, or from the remains of the exploiters' class. They have no place to go. So they take to—pederasty. Together with them, next to them, under this excuse, in stinky secretive little bordellos, another kind of activity takes place as well—counterrevolutionary work." Cited in Masha Gessen, *The Rights of Lesbians and Gay Men in the Russian Federation*, International Gay and Lesbian Human Rights Commission, 1994, p. 9.

[19] Interview by Razvan Ion and Scott Long with Imre Andras, member of the Romanian Chamber of Deputies, March 1993. Despite the restrictions on its mandate, Amnesty International took up several cases of persons falsely accused of homosexuality by Romanian authorities. These included Gheorghe Rusu, who was sentenced to three years'

A law wielded sporadically against ideological nonconformists, though, was enforced severely upon sexual dissidence—amid virtual indifference abroad. "Terrorism" is how one gay man describes it: "You never knew where they would strike, there was nobody you could completely trust."[20] One man imprisoned repeatedly for homosexuality recalls how arrests took place:

> In 1983, I was arrested for the first time. I brought a man home to my apartment, we had sex, and then he left. I don't know who reported us but they moved very fast. In the morning, before dawn, four policemen came to the apartment, broke in, and picked me up. I was sentenced to four years.[21]

Another gay man remembers:

> In 1988, when I was twenty-six, I went to see a friend who was renting a room in Bucharest, near Piata Rahova. There was another man who was living in the apartment. The three of us all had drinks; then my friend started showing us some porn magazines, gay and straight, which he had got from abroad. The third man left. Eventually my friend and I took our clothes off and got into bed, naked, in separate beds, looking at the magazines. We fell asleep.
>
> When we woke up, there were police, seven or eight of them, breaking down the door. The other man in the apartment had reported us. We were taken to the Section 17 police station and beaten over and over until we signed confessions that we had had homosexual sex. I was sentenced to two and one half years'

---

imprisonment on charges of "homosexual acts" as punishment for requesting to join his wife and child in France; and Mihail Botez, who applied to marry a French citizen and emigrate to France, and was sentenced to one year's imprisonment under Article 200 after what Amnesty International called "a carefully staged 'frame-up' by the state security police." *Amnesty International World Report*, 1980, pp. 291-92..

[20] Interview by Scott Long with Daniel Iorga, June 1997.

[21] Interview by Scott Long, Yves Nya Ngatchou, and Bogdan Voicu with Mihai Crismareanu, Braila Penitentiary, June 1997.

> imprisonment, and my friend—who owned the magazines—to three years.[22]

In imposing a total ban on private sexual activity, Article 200 suppressed not just any public development of gay or lesbian identity but the very acts and desires on which that identity might be based. Unlike measures restricting already extant ethnic or religious groups, Article 200 was a comprehensive effort to keep a new minority identity from breaking forth. The subterranean invisibility into which gay and lesbian sexuality was thereby driven—and in which, in large part, it continues to languish—renders documenting human rights violations based on sexual orientation extremely difficult. But in itself that invisibility violated basic rights, denying its victims voice, community, mutual contact, and self-understanding.

Same-sex sexual activity continued to take place in Romania, amid matrices of secrecy and mistrust. In the absence of bars or any other legal meeting places, gay men met surreptitiously, in places where they could go unnoticed, either in darkness or in a crowd. In almost every town, a park or railway station was quietly reclaimed as a cruising area. As one man explains, "Stations and parks were places where you could wait around, loiter, and speak to strangers, without arousing undue suspicion." Often sexual activity in these places, secluded by night, seemed safer than indoors. The same man says that taking a partner home could be dangerous:

> It wasn't just that your neighbors might see or hear. If you took someone home, he knew where you lived. If he was an informer, he could report you. Under bushes or in a toilet stall, even if you were caught, there was the chance that you could make a clean getaway. And if you did, maybe no one could find you.[23]

Few lesbians enjoyed even this measure of mobility. Both economic and social pressure constrained most women to marry early; nor, for most, were models or images available through which a lesbian identity could be constructed. Indeed, both women and men wrestling with homosexual feeling relied, to comprehend themselves, on any scraps of information they might find, building a mirror from shards with the glue of desperation. I.B., now a lesbian activist, remembers:

---

[22] Interview by Scott Long and Yves Nya Ngatchou with Mihai Tintila, Iasi Penitentiary, June 1997.

[23] Interview by Scott Long with E.M.,Cluj, May 1994.

> At the time, I did not even know that words such as 'lesbianism' or 'homosexuality' existed. In a closed society like pre-1989 Romania, the issue was more than a taboo: it simply did not exist. But I had been attracted to women from a very early age and was wondering . . . what was happening to me. I was lucky enough to get hold on the black market of a magazine featuring two women making love. I realized then that this was what I wanted, but I knew it was hard to get in a society where you have to pay with your freedom for being attracted to someone of the same sex as you.[24]

The regime made its own paranoia come true. Anathematizing homosexuality as a foreign influence, it ensured that chance flotsam of information from abroad was one of the few sources of identity left for lesbians and gays.

Under such conditions, survival itself was often at stake. The commandant of Galati penitentiary related one of his own experiences with the law to IGLHRC in 1993:

> Early on, I had a friend and classmate at the lyceum; later on he became lead dancer at the Galati state ballet. In the Seventies, he was arrested; there was a public scandal of some sort; very possibly he solicited an undercover officer. They slapped him with a prison sentence of quite a few years. As it happened he was put here in the penitentiary where I was already working.
>
> Before he was released I had an interview with him—that was the procedure. I asked him, "Why do you do these disgusting things, why do you want such things? You're an intelligent, educated man, an artist."
>
> He told me, "I don't have any choice about it. This is what is normal for me."

---

[24] Interview by Mona Nicoara with I.B., 1995; in Rachel Rosenbloom, ed., *Unspoken Rules: Sexual Orientation and Women's Human Rights,* International Gay and Lesbian Human Rights Commission, 1995, p. 165.

A year or so later, he was picked up again, under similar circumstances. He was set free pending trial. Before the trial began, he killed himself.[25]

[25] Interview by Razvan Ion and Scott Long with Col. Ion Zerca, Galati Penitentiary, January 1993.

3. ABUSE OF HOMOSEXUALS IN THE NEW ROMANIA

After Romania's violent change of government in December 1989, many of the most egregious Ceausescu-era laws affecting private life were struck down. Prohibitions on abortion were repealed within days of the National Salvation Front's pacification of the country. In some districts, it even appears that police lists of suspected homosexuals were discarded or lost. One policeman in Sibiu told IGLHRC in 1993, "After the Revolution, the police were intimidated and were not doing their jobs. Many of the old files on homosexuals had been destroyed. I had to begin rebuilding them virtually from scratch."[26]

However, Article 200 itself remained unchanged. The law only gradually began to attract international attention. The Romanian government responded to periodic questions by claiming that the first paragraph of the article, prohibiting consensual sexual relations between adults of the same sex, was a "dead law," no longer enforced.[27]

But these assertions were false. Other officials in the Ministry of Justice confirmed, at the same time, that persons convicted for homosexuality were still held in the prison system.[28] The International Gay and Lesbian Human Rights Commission was eventually able to document numerous abuses against the rights

---

[26] Interview by Razvan Ion and Scott Long with Lt. Mircea Mate, Sibiu, May 1993.

[27] Early in 1992 the International Gay and Lesbian Human Rights Commission (IGLHRC) conducted a fact-finding mission to Romania, accompanied by representatives of the International Lesbian and Gay Association (ILGA) and the European Council of AIDS Service Organizations (EUROCASO). Undersecretary of state Lucian Stingu of the Romanian Ministry of Justice confirmed that, so long as it remained on the books, any homosexual organization in Romania would be illegal, as a "threat to public order." However, he insisted to the mission that no prisoners were held under paragraph 1 of Article 200: all those imprisoned before 1989 had been freed in subsequent amnesties, he claimed, and the law was not being enforced. He promised that the paragraph would be repealed before "the next visit of representatives of your organizations." Interview by John Clark, Russ Gage, and Kurt Krickler with undersecretary Lucian Stingu, 1992; cited in Kurt Krickler, "Hoffnung in Rumanien," *LAMBDA Nachrichten*, July-August-September 1992, pp. 50-51.

[28] Letter from Adrian Duta, undersecretary of state in the Ministry of Justice, to Stefan Cooper, July 1992 ; interview by Razvan Ion and Scott Long with Adrian Duta, January 1993.

of lesbians and gay men in the Romania of the post-1989 era—cases which reveal the tenacity of prejudice among police, prosecutors, and other officials.

The Case of Ciprian Cucu and Marian Mutascu

In 1992, Ciprian Cucu, seventeen, was in the last year of high school in Sinnicolau Mare, a town near the Hungarian border. Isolated and lonely, in November 1992 he placed a personal advertisement in a Timisoara daily newspaper. The ad was titled "November dream"; in it, he asked to meet someone interested in "long-term friendship." The ad was subtly phrased to indicate his homosexuality.

The advertisement was answered by Marian Mutascu of Timisoara, twenty-two. Mutascu later said of their meeting, "I knew at once that this was the man and this was the way of life for me."[29]

They lived together for almost two months, at first staying in Mutascu's flat, which he shared with his mother; later, they moved to Cucu's family's home in Sinnicolau Mare. They were forced to hide their relationship from family members. Eventually, however, Cucu's older sister and her husband became suspicious. The sister herself reported their relationship to the police.

The two were arrested in January 1993. According to Cucu, "I was the first one to be interrogated. The investigators called me a 'whore' repeatedly. . . . Marian admitted everything during the interrogation. I tried to deny it, until I was shown my diary, which had been brought to the police by my sister. Then I realized that I would lose everything."[30]

From Sinnicolau Mare they were taken to Timisoara. "Many police officers gathered to laugh at us," Ciprian states.

> Then we were taken to the county police lockup. On finding out the reason why we had been arrested, the warden of the lockup (known as the "karate man") jumped on Marian, kicking him in the mouth and stomach. He continued to kick him even after Marian fell down and lost consciousness. I was only insulted and mocked repeatedly.

---

[29] Interview by Scott Long with Marian Mutascu, June 1993.

[30] This and other citations of Cucu's account are taken from Ciprian Cucu, testimony to the International Tribunal on Human Rights Violations Against Sexual Minorities, New York, October 1995 (available from the International Gay and Lesbian Human Rights Commission).

> Marian and I were separated. I was taken to the pre-trial detention ward for juveniles. My cell had six beds in which, during the two months I was incarcerated, up to sixteen suspects at a time slept. Before I came into the cell, officers told the supervising inmate[31] that a homosexual was going to be put in the room. As a result, he told me from the very start that I had to have sex with him if I did not want things to go very badly. At first I resisted, but after a few blows, I was forced to give in. It was the first time I was raped—but not the last. In the course of the following month, he forced me to have sex with other inmates as well, while the other colleagues watched the "show."

Mutascu was also raped and beaten repeatedly. At a hearing after thirty days' incarceration, Cucu told prosecutors that rape was widespread in the police lockup. "Upon my return to the lockup, the warden beat me up in the presence of around twenty inmates, because I had 'exposed the secrets of the lockup.'"

Mutascu was charged under Article 200, paragraph 2, for homosexual relations with a minor.[32] Cucu was charged under Article 200, paragraph 1 (and was tried as an adult).

An article in the journal of the Timisoara police described the case in detail, including the names, full addresses, and even photographs of the accused. Treating the guilt of the two as an established fact, it placed blame on the younger partner, Cucu, a "peril to society":

> [The case] has shocked the city, owing to its delicate nature and its divergence from the norm. Looking at the facts and taking into account the age of the accused, you remain shocked by what they were capable of. . . . [When arrested], the two did not admit the

---

[31] The supervising inmate or *sef de camera* is delegated by prison guards to maintain order within the cell. Not only do supervising inmates routinely abuse their authority, extorting sexual and material favors from cellmates, but such abuses are tolerated, condoned, and even actively encouraged by prison officials. The supervising inmate essentially serves as a surrogate employed by guards and other penitentiary staff in order to violate the rights of prisoners with impunity.

[32] The age of consent for women involved in heterosexual relations in Romania is fourteen; there is no age of consent for heterosexual men. Article 200, paragraph 2 at the time provided a penalty of two to seven years' imprisonment for same-sex relations with a partner under eighteen.

> incriminating act—sexual relations between persons of the same sex. But after the investigation and the forensic report, it was established that this was a typical case of homosexuality. Ciprian Cucu, the "little girl," was passive, while Milorad Mutascu was active. What an activity!
>
> It is painful that such things happen, that youngsters are cast adrift, freed from social control. Will there be repentance and reform, or a tragic ending and a fall into vice?[33]

A national newspaper picked up the story, publicizing their names across the country.[34]

During their first month in jail, both Cucu and Mutascu were forced to undergo a painful and humiliating medical examination of their genital and anal areas. "The forensic report said they could not prove I had had sex with another man," Cucu says. "But both the prosecutor and the forensic doctor insisted on discovering 'who was the active and who was the passive' in my relations with Marian."

Both Amnesty International and the Romanian Helsinki Committee moved to defend the two. Cucu was released from pre-trial detention after two months. Mutascu, however, was detained for another two months. After developing a severe

---

[33] Gigi Horodinca, "Anuntul misterios," *Tim-Polis,* February 1993. AIDS was used as a justification for the investigation. In February 1993, before the trial, Razvan Ion and Scott Long interviewed with the prosecutor in the case, Liviu Cretiu. He explained that the two were being held in pre-trial detention for "psychiatric evaluation, since their relationship was clearly abnormal." He also noted: "We suspect the older partner of infection with AIDS, and this is a danger to society, and he should not be on the streets." However, he revealed that Mutascu had neither received nor been offered an HIV test. Asked to justify his suspicions, Cretiu said, "The police are qualified to make this judgment, and they have made it and I accept it."

[34] Gheorghe Crisan, "Visul de noiembrie s-a spulberat brusc," *Tineretul Liber,* February 22, 1993. Other reporters encountered a hostile reception. "At the end of January," according to Cucu's testimony before the International Tribunal on Human Rights Violations Against Sexual Minorities, "we were visited by a journalist from Radio Timisoara. . . . During the visit the investigator told my parents that he would no longer allow the journalist to air shows that 'violate the criminal code by defending a crime.' He said he would make the reporter reveal the name of a man who, on [another] show, had admitted he was homosexual." This was confirmed in an interview by Razvan Ion and Scott Long with the reporter, Mioara Dan, February 1993.

and disfiguring skin infection on his legs and feet, he was finally released on May 22.

The two came to trial on June 9. Both were convicted; Mutascu received two years' imprisonment, and Cucu one year. Largely due to intensive pressure from the international community, these sentences were suspended.

Their ordeal was not over. Cucu was expelled from his school, "because teachers declared my homosexuality a danger to the other students." Employers, alerted by publicity, refused to hire Mutascu. When he managed to find a job, fellow workers' harassment drove him from it.

In May, 1995, Marian Mutascu committed suicide. Ciprian Cucu writes:

> He killed himself because he could not bear the pressure of isolation and fear. I had lived with the hope that one day we would stand together again. I loved him tremendously and could not believe I had lost him. But destiny took away this last hope. . . . A part of me went into the earth with him: what continues to live is surrounded by hatred and disgrace. It is too difficult to live in a society sick with prejudice, which condemns you for things that should carry no dishonor and cause no guilt.[35]

The Case of Costel Barbu, Mihaita Boghean, Cosmin Hutanu, Augustin Moldoveanu, and Mihai Vechiu

Cosmin Hutanu was nineteen when, in Focsani, a factory town north of Bucharest, he committed the act which led to his eventual imprisonment. One evening in 1991, he was invited to watch videos at the house of an acquaintance named Mihai Vechiu. Hutanu later told IGLHRC:

> He had an import-export business and he owned a video player, which was something hardly anyone in Focsani had ever seen. There were several other people in his house, watching rented movies. Later on he took me into another room where they couldn't hear, and he asked me if he could give me a blow job. I agreed.[36]

This one act was the only sexual contact between the men.

---

[35] Ciprian Cucu, testimony to the International Tribunal on Human Rights Violations Against Sexual Minorities.

[36] Interview by Scott Long, Yves Nya Ngatchou, and Bogdan Voicu with Cosmin Hutanu, Focsani penitentiary, January 1994.

Almost a year later, in July 1992, Vechiu made a similar offer to two other friends of Hutanu's, Costel Barbu and Augustin Moldoveanu. They too accepted.

Hutanu heard of this only later, through police interrogations. Vechiu lived with a woman who discovered the incident with Barbu and Moldoveanu, and reported it to the police.

On July 28, 1992, Focsani police arrested Vechiu, Barbu, and Moldoveanu, along with another man named Mihaita Boghean whom the woman also incriminated. According to Hutanu, the police initially tried to accuse Barbu and Moldoveanu of using force against Vechiu. Both men, though, knew about Hutanu's relations with Vechiu, and cited that old incident in their defense. Police promptly arrested Hutanu.

Hutanu told IGLHRC that police mocked him as a homosexual during an interrogation of several hours. They assured him, though, that he was only wanted as a witness and would not be charged. Hence he signed a statement detailing the one incident of the previous year, when Vechiu had performed oral sex on him.

Hutanu was conditionally released. In September he received a summons in which, despite police promises, he was listed as charged under Article 200, paragraph 1, facing five years in prison. Finally, in January 1993, Hutanu fled to Germany.

The trial of the five defendants—Hutanu, Vechiu, Boghean, Barbu, and Moldoveanu—had been postponed until the fall of 1992, apparently in part because of Hutanu's absence. It finally took place on February 24,1993, with Hutanu tried *in absentia.* Vechiu, Boghean, Barbu, and Moldoveanu were all convicted of consensual homosexual sex under Article 200, paragraph 1. They were sentenced to "correctional labor" in a workplace.[37]

Hutanu returned to Romania in June 1993, having decided to take his chances with the law. Within a month, police arrested him. Hutanu discovered that at the February trial he had been convicted and sentenced to one year and two months in prison, rather than at a workplace. Finally facing his legal punishment for a single sexual act, he was sent to Focsani penitentiary.

[37] As provided in Article 86 of the penal code, introduced in Law 6/1973. Hutanu's file in Focsani penitentiary, inspected by IGLHRC, did not indicate where these sentences were carried out or how long their durations were. Trial *in absentia* is provided for in Article 291 of the code of criminal procedure.

The Case of Ovidiu Banu, Lucian Blaga, Ovidiu Bozdog, Florin Hopris, Gheorghe Nastase, and Ciprian Stoica

In January and February 1993, police in the Transylvanian city of Sibiu began arresting suspected homosexuals. Five persons were eventually jailed, and charged under Article 200, paragraph 1. All were pressured to confess to sexual relations with a prominent newspaper publisher who appeared to be the target of the investigation, possibly for political motives. When enough evidence had been collected, police also arrested the publisher.

The investigation began when Nastase, nineteen and unemployed, was detained in January 1993 for riding a train without a ticket. While his arrest was unrelated to homosexuality, he was apparently already listed in police files as a homosexual.[38] While in custody, he was therefore pressured to name sexual contacts. He seems to have produced at least two names: Lucian Blaga, twenty-four, a marginal figure in Sibiu; and Ovidiu Bozdog, forty-one, publisher of a local newspaper.

Evidently Bozdog interested the police because he was a powerful, and wealthy, personality in the city. However, for precisely that reason a solid case against him would be necessary. Therefore, in early January, Lucian Blaga was also brought in. Blaga, according to Lt. Mircea Mate, the investigating officer in the case, had served at least one previous conviction under Article 200, paragraph 1. It appears that he named other homosexuals whom he suspected of contact with Bozdog. The police then started bringing in these men too.

Their arrests followed a common pattern. The first to be summoned was Ovidiu Banu, twenty-five, a puppet master at a theater in Sibiu. The investigating officer asked Banu about his relations with Gheorghe Nastase and demanded whether Banu were homosexual. Frightened, Banu acknowledged that he was. The investigating officer then read a long list of names, headed by Ovidiu Bozdog's, and asked if Banu had had sexual relations with them. Banu admitted to relations with Bozdog and with two other persons (Florin Hopris and Ciprian Stoica) who were later arrested.

The lieutenant told Banu that if he cooperated, he could go home—and invited him to give names of any "doctors, lawyers, army officers, politicians, or factory managers" in Sibiu who were homosexual. Banu refused. He was then taken to a hospital, where his genitals and anus were examined. (The prosecutor's file included a medical report showing "modifications to the penis indicating [Banu] has

[38] Interview by Razvan Ion and Scott Long with Lt. Mircea Mate, Sibiu, May 1993. In 1993-94 Ion, Long, and Bogdan Voicu visited Sibiu three times, interviewing Ovidiu Banu, Ovidiu Bozdog, Florin Hopris, and Ciprian Stoica, as well as Chief Prosecutor Ion Emrich, Lt. Mate, and other members of the police; most of this account is based on those interviews.

been an active partner in homosexual sex."[39]) Finally, he was charged under Article 200, paragraph 1.

His father was unable to raise bail for his son; Banu was held in pre-trial detention for over two months. He was isolated completely by the other prisoners after they discovered the charge against him, and one prisoner beat him and attempted to rape him.

On February 4, based on Banu's information, Lieutenant Mate summoned Florin Hopris, nineteen, a student at a private university in Sibiu.

The investigating officer was joined by a prosecutor, who read Banu's declaration implicating Hopris. (The prosecutor addressed him in the feminine gender.) Terrified, Hopris confessed to sexual relations with Banu, and with Ovidiu Bozdog. He was then shown a thick black album, full of photographs of men. Some—though not all—were police photographs taken at the time of arrest. He was told that these were suspected homosexuals, and interrogated about his relations with them.

He was released, but arrested three days later: handcuffed, taken to the hospital, and subjected to the same medical examination Banu had undergone. Held under Article 200, paragraph 1, he was placed in the police lockup. Hopris's mother sold her jewelry to raise his bail; he was freed after a week. His temples are touched with gray hair. When IGLHRC representatives asked about this, he responded, reluctantly, that it had turned gray during his time in jail.

On the same day Hopris was first questioned, Lieutenant Mate also brought Ciprian Stoica, twenty-one, a first-year university student, to the police station. Stoica denied having had sex with Florin Hopris; he was then questioned closely about his sexual relations with Ovidiu Bozdog—clearly the important person in the case—which Stoica admitted.

Like Banu, Stoica was asked to name any doctors, lawyers, politicians, or other prominent Sibiu personalities he knew to be homosexual. He was also shown the "black book," with photographs of suspected homosexuals. The investigating officer let Stoica go, with instructions to return on the following Monday. On that day, at the police station, he was handcuffed, subjected to a medical examination, and arrested under Article 200, paragraph 1.

He remained in jail for a month, since his parents were unable to raise bail.

Finally, when enough confessions had been collected, Ovidiu Bozdog was arrested on February 12, and told he had been implicated in homosexual relations by the other five suspects. The publisher denied all charges and declined to cooperate. When shown the "black book" with photographs of suspected

---

[39] File no. 5711/1993, judecatoria Sibiu.

homosexuals, he refused to look at it. According to Bozdog, Lieutenant Mate threatened his reputation, telling him, "I will have *Evenimentul zilei* [News of the Day—the largest national newspaper, and a venue for gossip and scandal] write about you."[40]

Bozdog was arrested under Article 200, paragraphs 1 and 2.[41] He spent a week in pre-trial detention before raising bail. He has asserted the case was launched against him on political grounds: at the time of his arrest he was preparing to launch an opposition newspaper.

The defendants were released, but for the next year and a half they faced the likelihood of trial and imprisonment. Their case eventually reached the Constitutional Court of Romania. Other newspapers in Sibiu publicized the case, to embarrass Bozdog. As a result, the other defendants suffered harassment as well. Ovidiu Banu was fired from his job, the principal support for his father as well as himself. (His father told IGLHRC, "I wish my son had died.") Children in the neighborhood threw stones at him when he walked the street, and their house was vandalized. The Hopris family's next-door neighbor called the police repeatedly, demanding to know why their son was not returned to jail.

Meanwhile, Lieutenant Mate proudly took personal responsibility for the "black book" in which names and photographs of suspected homosexuals were kept. Asked by IGLHRC in 1993 how many homosexuals the Sibiu police had on file, he answered, "Very many, extremely many."

The Case of Traian Pasca

In early 1993, two men in the Transylvanian town of Cugir broke into the home of another man, whom they believed to be homosexual. They robbed him and forced him to have sex with them. When the victim made an official complaint, prosecutors accused him of having wanted and solicited sexual relations with the two, a charge considered tenable since—as the police appeared to know—he was homosexual. The victim was then tried and convicted under Article 200.

When the events occurred, Traian Pasca, thirty-eight, was living in a workers' hostel in the town of Cugir. Pasca's court file[42] begins with his first, handwritten statement to the police. On the night of February 9, 1993, he states, Florin Musat

---

[40] Interview by Ion and Long with Ovidiu Bozdog, May 1993.

[41] Gheorghe Nastase and Florin Hopris had admitted to having had sex separately with Bozdog when each was seventeen, making them minors under Romanian law; see files no. 5298/1993, 5711/1993, and 5943/1993, judecatoria Sibiu.

[42] Dosar no. 3268/1993, judecatoria Alba Iulia.

and Dorin Foia broke down his door in the hostel. They took down their pants and demanded "*relatii secsuale (oral)*." Pasca says that he tried to alert the neighbors and to run away. However, Foia seized him "and put his penis in my mouth." Musat then did the same.

Pasca finally escaped; by the time he came back, the two were gone and his watch had been stolen.

Pasca states that they were drunk, and that they had had "abnormal sexual relations" with him twice in the past. He asks the police to take legal measures against them.

In 1994, IGLHRC interviewed Musat and Foia in Aiud penitentiary, where they were serving their sentences under Article 200. They confirmed this account. Pasca, an acquaintance, was known in town as a homosexual; drunk and passing his hostel, they decided to pay him a visit and "rough him up a bit."

Next morning, they were picked up by police on Pasca's complaint. Police found Pasca's watch on Musat. When they were taken to office of prosecutor Dana Ghitoaca, Pasca was also there, to face them as their accuser. However, a remarkable and disturbing series of events then happened through which the victim became a defendant in turn.

According to Musat, when he was arrested police informed him that Pasca had accused the two of raping him. They advised the two men to declare in their statements that Pasca had sex with them of his own free will; then, police told them, the two would be set free.

Police and prosecutor, clearly, were assembling a case against Pasca for committing homosexual acts. According to Musat, police wanted Pasca himself to withdraw his declaration and affirm that the sex was consensual. Getting declarations to this effect from the two assailants was the first step. The police wrote such declarations and Musat and Foia signed them. The three together were then taken before the prosecutor, who spent most of this session confronting not Foia and Musat but Pasca, accusing him of being a homosexual (Musat believes the police had prior information on Pasca[43]), and demanding to know why he did not try to run or resist when the two attempted to have sex with him. According to Musat, Pasca—intimidated—said nothing. The prosecutor then made out a mandate of arrest against Pasca.

---

[43] When IGLHRC representatives Scott Long and Yves Nya Ngatchou visited Cugir in April 1994—observing the still-smashed door of Pasca's domicile—his contemptuous neighbors indicated his homosexuality was well-known: "Everybody knew about him and the things he did," one said.

The file shows that the prosecutor charged Pasca under Article 200.[44] This is followed by a declaration from Pasca, dated February 11, 1993. This declaration is in a handwriting other than Pasca's (judging from the first declaration), though it appears to be signed by him. He states he had known Foia for ten years, Musat for five. In February 1992, a year before these events, they came together to his place and forced him to have oral sex. "I said nothing because I did not want to make problems for them, and I hoped it would not recur." In April 1992, the writer says, the same thing happened, and they had oral sex in the same way. "I may mention that they broke my door both times, but I cannot prove these things with a witness."

On the night of 9 February, they broke his door again. The remainder of the account roughly follows his previous statement.

To the authorities' frustration, Pasca was still insisting that he had been violently assaulted. Finally—as Musat said, "after they had bullied him enough"—he retracted this statement as well, at least in part, in ambiguous language which nonetheless admits "guilt." A third, much shorter declaration, also dated February 11, is typed. In it, Pasca acknowledges simply: "I recognize that I committed the infraction for which I am kept in custody, namely, sexual relations between persons of the same sex; I entered into sexual relations with Foia Dorin and Musat Florin"—although he adds, "but by force." A handwritten scrawl on the declaration, not written by Pasca, reads, "Start a penal action under Article 200."

On June 28, 1993, all three were tried in Alba Iulia. In addition to the charges of violation of domicile and theft leveled against Musat and Foia, all three were found guilty under Article 200 and sentenced to one year and six months under that charge. No paragraph of the article was specified during the trial, an apparent instance of judicial indifference or incompetence.[45]

Traian Pasca had been under pre-trial detention since February. He served his term until November, when he was finally paroled.

The Case of Ovidiu Chetea, Nicolae Petricas, and Nicolae Stupariu

In 1992, Ovidiu Chetea, an eighteen-year-old florist, was arrested in Timisoara. He claims his arrest was a pretext for the police to gain entry to his flat and arrest his roommates, who were suspected of homosexuality. Prosecutors charged Chetea and two of his roommates under Article 200, paragraph 1.

---

[44] No paragraph was specified. Article 4, paragraph 2 (defining a "continued and complex" infraction) was applied, apparently because Pasca had confessed to a previous experience with the two.

[45] Sentinta penala no. 1569/1993, judecatoria Alba Iulia; on file with Human Rights Watch and IGLHRC.

Their disturbing story exemplifies the invasiveness, and corruption, of a judicial system avid for evidence of private acts, as well as the brutality of prisons where the three underwent repeated beatings.

Chetea lived with Nicolae Petricas, twenty-four, and Nicolae Stupariu, thirty-one. All three (Chetea and Petricas later told IGLHRC) were gay; all worked at the main flower market in Timisoara. The exact circumstances of Chetea's arrest on March 13, 1992 remain unclear; his court file[46] deals exclusively with the accusation of homosexuality. He later received a suspended sentence for theft; Chetea says he was arrested for stealing flowers, but that police knew one of his roommates, Stupariu, was homosexual, and seized Chetea as an excuse to enter their flat and collect evidence.

The indictment ultimately produced in the case details what the police found at the flat; it exhibits as well the penetrability of private life in Romania. There were "various materials of a pornographic nature (videocassettes and magazines), exclusively depicting sexual relations between men, as well as a letter sent to the aforementioned accused by a person living in Holland (having emigrated from Romania) through which they were given these materials and the addresses of some homosexuals the defendants could contact in order to be able to emigrate." In addition, police confiscated Stupariu's address book, noting that it contained mostly male names. On this basis, Petricas and Stupariu were arrested. During interrogation, Petricas identified Ovidiu Chetea as one of his sexual contacts.

Chetea told IGLHRC that he was beaten severely by the police, because he refused to admit his homosexuality and to confirm his relations with Petricas. The beatings were so intense that he repeatedly lost consciousness.

Meantime, he says, Stupariu was beaten as well. Chetea contends that the beatings contributed to Stupariu's later death, in August 1993, apparently of an unidentified stomach disorder. Stupariu had seemingly refused to confess to his relations with a person identified in the prosecutor's report as "Adi" from Deva, with whom he had allegedly had sexual relations in the city of Hunedoara in August 1991. One persistent question in this case is how the police had obtained this information. A possibility raised by Chetea is that "Adi" was an informer who had given the police Stupariu's name—lending credence to the possibility that Chetea was detained for theft in order to gain more evidence against Stupariu.

---

[46] Dosar no. 5856/1993, judecatoria Timisoara. Copies of most documents on file with Human Rights Watch and IGLHRC. In March 1994 Scott Long, Yves Nya Ngatchou, and Aurelian Seres visited Timisoara and interviewed Nicolae Petricas and Ovidiu Chetea; this account is largely based on their stories. Nicolae Stupariu, by that time, was dead. See also Anca David, "Un tanar homosexual a fost torturat de puscariasi," *Libertatea,* July 15, 1996.

Prosecutors rejected Stupariu's denials. "We consider the formulations of the defendant irrelevant," the report notes, citing Stupariu's ownership of the cassettes and magazines in the flat as evidence that he was a confirmed homosexual. The indictment also cites evidence given by another roommate, who told police that the defendants had made effeminate gestures to one another and had only been visited by other men.

Petricas and Stupariu were kept under arrest for one month. They were both freed, according to Petricas, when they paid bribes of one hundred DM (approximately U.S. $75 at the time) each to have their pre-trial detention warrants canceled. Ovidiu Chetea remained detained for four months.

Petricas and Chetea both report that they were beaten and raped by their cellmates, who numbered over sixty. They believe that this took place with the knowledge of the guards, who had made a point of identifying them to the other prisoners as homosexuals. And, in one incident recounted by Petricas, as they were lining up naked to go to the showers, one of the prison guards demanded to know which were the homosexuals. He then separated Chetea, Stupariu, and Petricas, and beat them with a wooden club.

On the night before Petricas and Stupariu were freed, the guards announced their impending departure to the other prisoners. The two were then forced to have sex with the entire cell-group—or rather, were shared out, with half taking Stupariu, half Petricas. In a trial on June 26, 1992, Petricas (who was charged with having repeatedly broken Article 200, paragraph 1) was sentenced to two years in prison. Chetea received a year and six months for the same charge; Stupariu, who was charged only with the one "crime" with "Adi" in August 1991, received one year. Petricas's and Stupariu's sentences were suspended—because, Petricas claims, they paid further bribes to the court. Chetea's sentence was not.

In December 1992, the prosecutor appealed this decision, asking that Stupariu and Petricas be imprisoned, and calling attention to the gravity of their crimes and the "social threat" they represented. On February 8, 1993—a year after the ordeal began—this appeal was rejected by the Timisoara court.[47]

---

[47] Chetea benefited for a time from the incompetence of the authorities. A document found in a file in the courthouse in the distant city of Oradea (dosar no. 6819/1993; copies of contents on file with Human Rights Watch and IGLHRC) indicates that, on July 15, 1992—while he was serving his Article 200 sentence—his theft case came to trial in Timisoara, and he was given one year's imprisonment—suspended. This suspension should not have affected his imprisonment for homosexuality. However, in what was either a judicial bungle or a highly irregular act, on July 17, he was set free.

He was picked up again in Oradea, in March 1993; the file in Oradea states that he was stealing flowers from a cemetery.

4. UNDER PRESSURE FROM EUROPE

Revising Article 200

Article 200 unexpectedly became a barrier to the main priority—integrating the country into European institutions—of Romania's post-revolutionary governments. Rapporteurs from the Council of Europe, visiting Romania in April 1993 to investigate its human-rights record after it applied for admission, raised the issue of homosexuality. The government responded:

> It is true that sexual relations between people of the same sex are a punishable offence under Article 200 of the Romanian Criminal Code . . . In pursuance of this text, a number of people are at present serving prison sentences for homosexuality. . . .
>
> It must be said, however, that total decriminalisation of homosexuality would not seem possible at present, since acts of this kind are alien to the Romanian people's mentality, and offend the general moral feeling and religious conscience of the great majority of the population.[48]

Oradea prosecutors contacted the Timisoara court, which informed them of Chetea's sentence for homosexuality. Attempting to cover up the irregularity of his release, however, Timisoara offered no information on why the sentence had not been served.

Chetea then remained in detention for nine months without trial. He was kept there by the prosecutors and court in Oradea, who tried repeatedly and unsuccessfully to obtain word from Timisoara on whether his previous sentence had been amnestied or fulfilled.

In November 1993, the Romanian Helsinki Committee had received from the Ministry of Justice a list of persons imprisoned for homosexuality. Ovidiu Chetea appeared on this list. On December 20, IGLHRC representatives received permission from the Ministry of Justice to visit him in Oradea penitentiary. IGLHRC arrived at the penitentiary on December 22, to find he had been released the day before.

It seems possible that he had been freed in order to hide the details of his case, as well as the series of judicial errors by which the Oradea court—abetted by the stonewalling of authorities in Timisoara—kept him in prison for nine months, while having no clear information on what previous crime he was being held for.

[48] Parliamentary Assembly of the Council of Europe, Committee on Legal Affairs and Human Rights, "Draft opinion on the application for membership to the Council of Europe submitted by Romania," appendix II, AS/Jur (44) 74, Strasbourg, August 17, 1993. See also AS/Pol 44(62), Strasbourg, May 7, 1993.

Even before the rapporteurs' visit, attempts to discuss Article 200 in parliament had led to uproar. In February 1993, when the article was mentioned in a debate on provisions against prostitution, Senator Emil Tocaci indignantly proposed that male homosexuals should be kept in women's penitentiaries, and vice-versa.[49] The very possibility that Romania's admission to the Council of Europe might hinge on repeal of the law, though, produced a storm. One nationalist newspaper advised the government to hang out a "fluorescent signboard" with the legend "Homo-sex-rom-euro-club."[50]

Mainstream figures concurred. Corneliu Coposu, leader of the Christian Democrats (PNTCD), the largest opposition party, pledged to "fight sexual aberrations":

> The Christian moral conception which remains the basis of our party's doctrine leads us to combat every deviation from the law of nature and from the moral principles of a future balanced society. Without hesitation, in debating this point of American inspiration, we give the word that we are categorically opposed . . . We contend that liberty must be blocked by the liberty of others—when the collective sentiment of a group or a tradition is injured by some initiative pretending to be "progressive" and modern, we must oppose it . . .[51]

The then Minister of Justice, Petre Ninosu, contributed what became a catch-phrase and cliche: "One of the most discussed passages of the penal code is Article 200, which punishes the animals who practice homosexual relations. This article has not been repealed, which seems to me quite normal. If we let homosexuals do as they

---

[49] Daniel Uncu, "La ordinea zilei in Senat: proxeneti, prostituate, homosexuali, lesbiene, si SIDA." *Romania libera,* February 7, 1993; and Tudor Octavian, "Senatorul Tatu si problema preacurviei," *Romania libera,* February 15, 1993. See also Abafai F. Istvan, "Andras Imre kepviselo: nem a tiltas a megoldas," *Orient expressz,* March 12, 1993.

[50] Nicolae Veres, "Domnul Konig, homosexualii, si . . . noi," *Adevarul de Cluj,* May 15-17, 1993.

[51] Roxana Costache, "Dl. Coposu combate aberatiile sexuale," *Libertatea,* May 18-19, 1993.

please, it would mean entering Europe from behind. Homosexuals are our last problem."[52]

Voting in September 1993 to admit Romania, the Council of Europe's Parliamentary Assembly imposed a simultaneous mandate, in two amendments to the resolution, to "discontinue the punishment of homosexuals."[53] The Romanian government half-complied. It finally brought before parliament a proposal to amend Article 200, paragraph 1: this reached back nearly sixty years to resuscitate an old phrase from the 1936 penal code, punishing "sexual relations between persons of the same sex, *if producing public scandal,*" with 1-5 years' imprisonment. Paragraph 5 would also be changed to punish "inciting or encouraging a person, *in public,* to commit the acts referred to in preceding paragraphs" with 1-5 years' imprisonment.[54]

Adding urgency, in July 1994 the Constitutional Court ruled on the Sibiu case, involving the defendants Banu, Blaga, Bozdog, Hopris, Nastase, and Stoica, as discussed above. After intense international pressure, the court found the existing language of Article 200 violated protections for privacy in Article 26 of the Romanian Constitution.[55] It allowed the law, however, to continue to punish homosexual acts "committed in public" or (without attempting to define the term) "causing public scandal."

Public opinion probably ensured that the debate over Article 200 would be heated. One survey in 1993 showed that 85 percent of respondents held that homosexual acts were "never justified."[56] But the argument went on for three years,

---

[52] Tana Cafrita, "Homosexualii se pot organiza in asociatia fara a fi pedepsiti de lege," *Evenimentul zilei,* April 6, 1993.

[53] Council of Europe, Parliamentary Assembly, Doc. 6901, Amendment No. 7, September 27, 1993. Amendment No. 8 also required that Romania "shortly change its legislation in such a way that . . . Article 200 of the penal code will no longer consider as a criminal offense homosexual acts perpetrated in private between consenting adults."

[54] The 1968 code paragraph 5 had criminalized "incitement or encouragement" only to the acts in paragraph 1, omitting incitement to the acts specified in the intervening paragraphs.

[55] Decizia nr. 81, Curtea Constitutionala, July 15, 1994.

[56] Survey by the Quality of Life Institute at the Romanian Academy. In "Homosexuals: premises of their acceptance in today's Romania," unpublished paper by Catalin Augustin Stoica.

during which all penal code reform was held hostage. Two influences particularly extended and intensified the agony: those of the Orthodox Church and of the media.

As one member of parliament told Human Rights Watch and IGLHRC, "The Orthodox Church has been more dogmatic with respect to this issue than in almost any other. . . . They were looking for an issue to use. Perhaps it might have been abortion, but the public sentiment against the old abortion laws made that dangerous to press. So they pressed homosexuality."[57] Most religious leaders in Romania opposed any changes in the law[58]; but the Orthodox Church's interventions were uniquely vociferous. Patriarch Teoctist regularly condemned, in statements read at services throughout Romania, "the acceptance of the degradingly abnormal and unnatural as a natural and legal lifestyle."[59] The church's share of religious programming on state TV was repeatedly turned over to attacks on altering Article 200. An association of seminary students, *Asociatia Studentilor Crestin-Ortodocsi din Romania* (ASCOR), organized a huge petition to the president and parliament, blasting homosexuality as "propaganda of human degenerates."[60] According to Dan Martian, then president of the Chamber of Deputies:

> During the debate ASCOR bombarded the deputies with information, petitions, and appeals, which all the took the line of criminalizing homosexuality, accusing those who wanted to decriminalize it of immorality or atheism . . . In several electoral districts deputies had to face groups from the populace who asked how decriminalizing

---

[57] Interview by Daniel Iorga, Scott Long, and Bogdan Voicu with Deputy Nicolae-Florin Tudose, July 1997.

[58] In its deliberations in 1994, the Constitutional Court had polled the officially recognized religions; all declared themselves against any amendment, with the sole exception of Bishop Laszlo Tokes of the Hungarian Reformed Church, who distinguished between the spheres of religious dogma and political decisions. Decizia nr. 81, Curtea Constitutionala, July 15, 1994.

[59] Ion Zubascu, "Patriarhul Romaniei condamna legiferarea homosexualitatii," *Evenimentul zilei,* December 16, 1993.

[60] *Homosexualitatea: propaganda a degenerarii umane*, pamphlet produced by ASCOR, 1995.

> homosexuality could be squared with the Christian traditions of the Romanian people.[61]

Almost all the government officials interviewed by Human Rights Watch and IGLHRC cited the role of the Orthodox Church in the debate—from legislators down to the local prosecutor who observed that "obviously, our point of view is guided by the Church in these matters."[62] A Christian Democratic member of parliament explained:

> In my personal opinion, you must consider some cultural and historical patterns. If the Catholic Church was an institution above all states, and if the Reformed Church started from a firm doctrine of separation from political life, the Orthodox Church was always an instrument of the state. Even under Communism—in Russia, elsewhere, and also here—it was used as a strong state tool. Many priests were also in the state services, and not a few worked for the Securitate. Now, of course, they are operating independently; they make their own policy. But they will not give up the benefits, or the connections they feel they should have to the state, easily.[63]

The mass media, particularly print journalism, also exploited the topic. "Vice remains the first step to crime," one national newspaper trumpeted even as the Council of Europe rapporteurs framed their questions to the government. Among the hundreds of papers that had mushroomed after 1989, many relied on crime reporting to boost sales. The fact that homosexuality was still illegal made it easy

---

[61] Interview by Vera Campeanu and Scott Long with Deputy Dan Martian, 1997.

[62] Interview by Scott Long and Bogdan Voicu with Chief Prosecutor Vasile Luha, Alba Iulia, 1997.

[63] Interview with Deputy Nicolae-Florin Tudose, July 1997. An discussion with three officials from the Ministry of Justice revealed that even there some confusion remains about the official status of the Orthodox Church, with one maintaining that Romania has an "official religion," and another stating (correctly) that the majority church is only one of the officially recognized churches, which at least in principle retain formal equality: interview by Vera Campeanu and Scott Long with Ana Iacovescu (Director of International Legal Relations), Cristina Lazarescu, and Colonel Radu Moldovan, Ministry of Justice, June, 1997.

to connect it to the category of violent crime. The murder of a popular musician, Ioan Luchian Mihalea, in late 1993, cemented the association. Police revealed that Mihalea was gay, and his death—an act of brutal violence practiced on a homosexual—was replayed luridly and incessantly in the press as a "homosexual murder." Before 1989, "homosexuals did not officially exist. Then appeared scandals and criminality," one newspaper declared, under the headline, "Homosexuals commit ferocious crimes."[64] Homosexuality was also tied demagogically to the sexual abuse of children. (Deputy Gheorghe Stancov told Human Rights Watch and IGLHRC that, in 1996, "at the same time we were debating the law, a huge scandal involving pedophilia erupted in Belgium. The press it received was very bad for the homosexual cause here." Reminded that the Belgian crime—like most cases of child abuse—involved the heterosexual abuse of girls, he observed, "Unfortunately, in Romania, that is a nuance.")[65]

Finally, both the extremist press and more mainstream journalists used the connection with the Council of Europe to play on nationalist sentiment, identifying homosexuality as a corrupt incursion alien to indigenous values. Let Europe have its way, one journalist warned, and "the whole country will be a house of tolerance [brothel] . . . while the West advances to Sodom and Gomorrah."[66] "If Western gentlemen embrace abnormality, let them, it's their problem," another intoned. "If this Council of Europe is composed of homosexuals, good riddance to them, and their whole Europe too."[67]

---

[64] Valentin Zaschievici and Cosmin Barbii, "Crimele oribile comise in ultimul timp in mediul homosexualilor ingrozesc Bucurestiul," *Libertatea*, November 9, 1995. See also (among others) Miruna Munteanu, "Crimele comis de homosexuali," *Zeghea*, August 13-19, 1996; "Oameni din umbra societatii: homosexualii," *Romania libera,* March 2, 1996; and "Homosexualii la Paris si la Bucuresti," *Zig Zag*, May 1993—all full-page spreads devoted to supposed "homosexual crimes." Soon an entire book on "rapes and homosexual murders," allegedly written by a former prosecutor, appeared: Ion Argesanu, *Atentie! Violatori si homosexuali ucigasi!* Oscar Print, Bucuresti, 1995.

[65] Interview by Vera Campeanu and Scott Long with Deputy Gheorghe Stancov, Judiciary Committee, Chamber of Deputies, June 1997.

[66] Nicolae Corbu, "Sex si politica," *Ultima ora,* spring 1993.

[67] "Isabelle si homosexualitatea," *Mesagerul*, July 3, 1993. Deputy Emil Teodor Popescu, interviewed by Vera Campeanu and Scott Long in June 1997, expressed nostalgia for an era when all borders—national as well as psychological—were sealed against transgressions and foreign influences: "Communism was very bad, but it had positive effects: pornography, drugs, rock music, AIDS. homosexuality were not seen or discussed and were

Discussions of Article 200 in parliament often skirted hysteria. “Where,” one senator demanded, “are those Romanians who conquered the world through the proper use of their sexual organs?”[68] The first vote of the Senate Judiciary Committee on the issue, in November 1993—just after the Mihalea murder—actually increased penalties for most paragraphs of the article[69]; and in October 1994, with only twelve votes dissenting, the Chamber of Deputies voted to retain the existing language, defying European objections as well as the Constitutional Court. One observer reports, “The mere mention of the Council of Europe generated booing and cursing in the hall.”[70] Later and more soberly, the chamber revisited the vote, and both houses accepted the public scandal language for inclusion in an omnibus bill of penal code revisions. However, in late 1994, this omnibus bill itself was voted down. The government's parliamentary majority depended on three extreme nationalist parties; these deserted the government, claiming the bill's partial liberalization of homosexual activity struck at national honor. An entire Ceausescu-era document was left intact because of one contested provision.

Dan Martian, a leader of the governing party, told Human Rights Watch and IGLHRC, “When the penal code failed, it created huge problems for us. We had to confront this very unpleasant loss of face. We were preoccupied with devising a way to pass the penal code revisions after that.”[71] The same farce, though, was replayed in the 1995 parliamentary session: again the entire package of penal code changes failed because it modified Article 200.

The article became linked with several other proposed penal code provisions, which would ban “transmission of false news,” increase penalties for slander, and prohibit the display of foreign flags. All were brainchildren of a government still seeking to control and constrict, where possible, the public sphere. But, Martian

---

eliminated from the start.”

[68] Peter Humphrey, “Gay Rights Cause Uproar in Romanian Parliament,” Reuters, November 11, 1993.

[69] It is worth noting that only deputies from Petre Roman's opposition Democratic Party (FSN) dared produce a legislative proposal, formally introduced in 1993, that would have eliminated Article 200, paragraph 1 altogether. The proposal rapidly died.

[70] Letter to Scott Long from Mona Nicoara of the Romanian Helsinki Committee, October 16, 1994.

[71] Interview by Campeanu and Long with Dan Martian, June 1997.

says, "With these articles it was easier to reach agreement than with 200. Opposition to altering 200 was inflexible, adamant, and we could not reach a consensus." The other proposals were criticized as too harsh; Article 200 was condemned as too indulgent. One legislator combating the changes called Article 200 "the Gordian knot of the penal code."[72]

In 1996, only a few weeks before national elections, the governing party at last succeeded in passing the omnibus bill. Martian says, "in the pre-election atmosphere certain deputies would not take the risk of voting against the entire penal code a third time." The final debate took place at frenzied pitch. Deputy Emil Teodor Popescu of the Christian Democrats, one of the most strident opponents of modification, declared incest preferable to homosexuality, because it at least preserved the chance to procreate. Another deputy said: "At this time, the interest of society must prevail over the rights of the individual. This is not the moment to accord individual liberty."[73]

The law as finally passed was officially promulgated on November 14, 1996. The new paragraph 1 penalizes consensual, adult homosexual relations with one to five years' imprisonment under two conditions: when "committed in public," or "if producing public scandal." A new paragraph 5 included language criminalizing "propaganda or association or any other act of proselytism" for same-sex sexual relations, further restricting freedoms of expression and assembly for lesbians and gays. The full text of the new article reads:

> 1. Sexual relations between persons of the same sex, committed in public or if producing public scandal, are punishable by imprisonment of one to five years.
>
> 2. The act of a major having sexual relations with a minor of the same sex is punishable by imprisonment of two to seven years and denial of certain rights.
>
> 3. Sexual relations with a person of the same sex incapable of defending him/herself or of expressing volition, or through force, are

---

[72] Emil Teodor Popescu, quoted in Lia Bejan and Dragos Moldovan, "Presa n-a scapat de inchisoare," *Adevarul*, 11 September 1996.

[73] Both quoted in Aura Alexa Ioan, "Cea mai aberanta pledoarie!", *Tinerama,* September 17-23, 1996.

punishable by imprisonment of three to ten years and denial of certain rights.

4. If the acts described in paragraphs 2-3 result in grave damage to bodily integrity or health, the punishment is imprisonment from five to fifteen years and denial of certain rights; if they result in the death or suicide of the victim, the punishment is imprisonment of fifteen to twenty-five years and denial of certain rights.

5. Inciting or encouraging a person to the practice of sexual relations between persons of the same sex, as well as propaganda or association or any other act of proselytism committed in the same scope, is punishable by imprisonment of one to five years.

The Concept of Public Scandal

From the moment in 1993 when the Romanian government moved to revise Article 200, it presented its proposal as fully adherent to European norms.

Others, however, disagree. Amnesty International has held that "'causing a public scandal' is such a broad term it could lead to varying and contradictory judicial interpretations."[74] One expert witness consulted by the Chamber of Deputies' Judiciary Committee called the term "an artificial notion, judicially unconvincing, marked by hypocrisy and repressive ideology"[75]; another commentator calls it "scandalously imprecise."[76] The term is, as one prosecutor observes, "completely undefined in the penal code"[77]—although it occurs in two

---

[74] Amnesty International Index: Eur 39/WU 02/94

[75] "Rezumatul sedintei Comisei Juridice a Camerei Deputatilor din 04.27.94": notes taken by representatives of the Romanian Helsinki Committee. The General Prosecutor's office defined the term for the same committee (without citing a precedent) as "the circumstance of the act becoming known to three people who show disapproval."

[76] Valerian Cioclei, *Viata sexuala si politica penala*, Bucuresti, Editura Holding Reporter, 1994, p. 91. A recently published dictionary of useful legal terms (co-authored by the head of the General Inspectorate of Police—IGP) devotes an entry to "homosexuality," a word nowhere mentioned in the penal code, but none to "public scandal": Dr. Ion Pitulescu, Dr. Pavel Abraham, Emil Dersidan, and Ion Ranete, *Dictionar de Termeni Juridici Uzuala, Explicativ-Practic*, Bucuresti, Editura National, 1997.

[77] Interview by Scott Long and Bogdan Voicu with Vasile Luha, July 1997.

other articles inherited unchanged from 1968: Article 201, dealing with "sexual perversion," and Article 321, both discussed below. Senator Peter Eckstein told Human Rights Watch and IGLHRC that the term is "a chewing-gum notion: you can stretch it any way you like. But it's a charge that can stick."[78]

The law seems aimed at public behavior. Yet its context is a country where private life was virtually eradicated over four decades. Emil Teodor Popescu—a fierce opponent of leniency toward homosexuality—observes, "Westerners cannot understand how difficult it is to speak of private life here. Nothing was private, everything was public."[79] Officials who spoke to Human Rights Watch and IGLHRC repeatedly stressed the tenuousness of privacy in post-Ceausescu Romania, and the fragility of legal protections for it. A crucial question, therefore, is whether the new law can be used against acts committed in supposed or seeming privacy. Because the law is so new, few cases exist so far to indicate how it will be interpreted; the opinions of officials are the best available guide to its future use. Those opinions are strikingly, and dangerously inconsistent, on many points. On whether the law can be enforced against acts performed in privacy, however, both those who created the law and those who will enforce it agree that it can.

Gen. Ovidius Paun of the General Inspectorate of Police (IGP) in the Ministry of Interior told Human Rights Watch and IGLHRC:

> What we understand by public scandal is any action that arouses the citizens, even if not done in public, but if done in conditions that cause public indignation. Suppose that two people of the same sex enter into relations in a room, but in view of a window, so that people passing in the street can see. Obviously the people will stop, make negative comments. In this condition we say the action raises the indignation of the public.[80]

Senator Ion Vasile of the Senate's Human Rights Commission suggested that scandal need not even be triggered by specific sexual acts—those could be inferred simply from the fact of a person's homosexuality:

---

[78] Interview by Vera Campeanu and Scott Long with Senator Peter Eckstein, June 1997.

[79] Interview by Vera Campeanu and Scott Long with Emil Teodor Popescu, Chair, Judiciary Committee, Chamber of Deputies, June 1997.

[80] Interview by Vera Campeanu and Scott Long with Gen. Ovidius Paun, IGP, June 1997.

> In a bloc of flats where twenty families live, say, one of the people is known to be homosexual. The majority will not accept this. They are very concerned about living in the same bloc with this kind of person. There is concern because most of these people have children, who might be molested, might adopt this person's way of living. . . Scandal doesn't necessarily mean a scandal in the juridical sense; it means also that problems of some sort already begin. Popular concern could constitute a scandal. . . . We are trying to make it possible to exclude that man from the community as a danger to it.[81]

A legal expert to the same committee said public scandal would exist if, "in a bloc of flats where there are many people, children, families, things happen in one apartment that disturb the neighbors—be it obscene words, things that contradict moral principles, people who are seen naked or half-naked." And Capt. Tudor Cojocaru of the Brasov police offered a concrete example of a case from 1995:

> There were two men, both married. The wife of one caught the two of them in the bedroom, in the act of having sexual relations, and she created a public scandal. She told the neighbors; she came to us, and insisted that we do something. We launched an investigation, because we couldn't get rid of her. The two admitted that they had homosexual relations, and ultimately were sentenced.[82]

Protections for privacy thus seem vulnerable at best, and further attenuated by social and cultural conditions which breed contempt for it. As Senator Vasile said, "Relationships between people living in the same bloc are extremely intimate; their lives are transparent, whereas in the West you may not know your neighbor." And a Ministry of Justice official observed that "Our legal system is waiting for the development of a respect for private life which has not existed before."[83]

---

[81] Interview by Vera Campeanu and Scott Long with Senator Ion Vasile, June 1997.

[82] Interview by Daniel Iorga, Scott Long, and Bogdan Voicu with Capt. Tudor Cojocaru, Brasov, July 1997. In 1995 the Constitutional Court had already pronounced its decision legitimating the "public scandal"language, though its legal force was uncertain. Human Rights Watch and IGLHRC were unable to obtain access to the file on this case in the judecatoria in Brasov.

[83] Interviews by Campeanu and Long with Senator Vasile, and with Ana Iacovescu, June 1997.

At same time, General Paun contended, "Public scandal depends on *willing* that an action be made public. The perpetrator must have the express intention that it can be heard or seen." Deputy Lupu confirmed this: "Public scandal in my view is a deliberate act of a person intending to create public scandal." However, Vasile Luha, chief prosecutor in Alba Iulia, told Human Rights Watch and IGLHRC, "There are no limitations: the act can come to the awareness of the public by any means. The revelation does not need to be willed or intended."[84] As long ago as 1993, a police official told IGLHRC that public scandal could be created by a homosexual couple who "make too much noise."[85]

The new language effectively makes it impossible to determine whether an act constitutes an infraction until *after* it is committed and publicized: the offense consists less in the specific character of the deed, or in its motive, than in others' reactions to it. Opinion rather than evidence becomes the final arbiter of guilt. "Our criterion is the mentality of the community where the deed is committed," one prosecutor said, adding, "our community of course does not view this phenomenon with favorable eyes."[86] The language even points to the possibility that the authorities themselves can create, then confirm, public scandal by publicizing the details of a case. For example: in one court sentence (under Article 201) from 1993, the arrest was justified post-facto, and "public scandal" was discovered, in "a sentiment of repulsion and revulsion . . . evident in expressions of public protest, *immediately upon the publication of information in the local press*"—information which could only have come from law enforcement officials themselves.[87]

Yet a curious numbers game sets the rules for what constitutes a "public." Prosecutor Luha commented: "To 'come to the knowledge of the public,' it is enough to have a few people from the immediate circle in which the persons live comment negatively on the acts." Prosecutor Evgenia Varvescu of Iasi said that "a minimum of three persons must express indignation." a police officer pegged the

---

[84] Interviews by Campeanu and Long with Paun and Lupu, June 1997; interview by Long and Voicu with Luha, July 1997.

[85] Interview by Scott Long with Capt. Dorel Andras, Timisoara Police, May 1994.

[86] Interview with Luha. Acting Chief Prosecutor Evgenia Varvescu in Iasi claimed that "the public is in fact more repressive and severe than the authorities, since it is grounded in Christian Orthodox morality." Interviewed by Scott Long and Bogdan Voicu, June 1997.

[87] Sentinta penala 02.03.1993, cazul Radu Alexandru, Tribunal Militar, Bucuresti. Most of the officials IGLHRC and Human Rights Watch interviewed found this an unacceptable procedure.

minimum at "two or more." And a prosecutor in Constanta identified public scandal as "when the act becomes known to someone else, even one single person, who objects." The chief inspector of police in Constanta agreed: it happens "when anyone finds out, pure and simple."[88]

Understandably, many officials were anxious to pass on responsibility for putting these definitions in order. Mariana Valeriana Stoica, of the Chamber of Deputies, maintained: "Defining public scandal is a matter for lawyers and not for parliamentarians." a Ministry of Justice official held, "It is people working on a practical level in the criminal justice system who will decide the meaning of the term."[89] Even those people, however, may approach the phrases gingerly. One prosecutor insisted that he has "no definition of public scandal," and that "only trials will decide an interpretation."[90]

Officials spoke of the new law as a "balance" between "protecting a minority, but protecting the majority as well." "We tried to sweeten the punishment as much as possible," Deputy Popescu said.[91] These protections seem slight at best. As for

---

[88] Interviews with Luha and Varvescu; interviews by Vera Campeanu and Scott Long with prosecutor Mariana Vutcovici, and with Colonel Ioan Cirlic, Constanta, June 1997.

[89] Interview by Vera Campeanu and Scott Long with Mariana Valeriana Stoica, President, Parliamentary Committee for European Integration; and with Cristina Lazarescu, Ministry of Justice, June 1997.

[90] Interview by Scott Long and Bodgan Voicu with Assistant Chief Prosecutor Ilie Costica, Braila, 1997. In practice, power in the Romanian judicial system is concentrated in the prosecutor rather than the judge: prosecutors approve and direct investigations, achieve a conviction rate of over 95 percent, and often see their bills of indictment transformed unedited into penal sentences. Hence prosecutors (who, based on Human Rights Watch's and IGLHRC's interviews, seem to interpret "public scandal" more broadly even than many legislators) are likely to have the predominant influence in any future jurisprudence.

[91] Interviews with Iacovescu and Popescu. Popescu, who is now the chair of the Judiciary Committee in the Chamber of Deputies, and who over the last three years was one of the most vociferous opponents of reforming Article 200—appearing in many programs and publications sponsored by the Orthodox Church—was anxious to present himself as more moderate in a meeting with Human Rights Watch and IGLHRC in June 1997 . He even contended, "This law helps homosexual couples. For it will encourage heterosexual couples to have more children. And later, when Romania is ready for such a thing, homosexual couples can adopt those children—which will be a favor to them, because

the assertion that "homosexuals are only imprisoned if certain limits are overpassed," it remains impossible to fix exactly what those limits are.[92]

"In Public"

Article 152 of the Romanian penal code reads:

> An act is considered performed in public when it was committed:
> a) in a place which by nature or purpose is always accessible to the public, even if no person is present;
> b) in any other place accessible to the public, if two or more persons are present;
> c) in a place inaccessible to the public, with the intention that the act be heard or seen, and if this result is produced in the presence of two or more persons;

---

homosexuality is essentially sterile."

[92] Interview with Iacovescu. Since 1993, the phrase "public scandal" has been widely disseminated in Romania; prosecutors often invoked it, as a precautionary measure, in Article 200 cases initiated well before the new law passed. However, several cases show that some prosecutors are unaware (even after the final promulgation of the law) that "public scandal" delimits only paragraph 1; they summon up the language in cases involving other paragraphs, with the curious result that even homosexual rape must be found to produce "public scandal." (The ease of doing so, of course, suggests again the elasticity of the term.) In one case under Article 200, paragraph. 3 (rechizitoriu 28/P/1997, dosar 291/1997, judecatoria Teleorman), in which a rape was committed outside a restaurant, the prosecutor finds "acts of homosexuality committed by force upon the victim, *which produced public scandal. That these acts produced public scandal is proven by the declarations of witnesses, who observed on that evening that persons in the restaurant were revolted, and again in following days when the act committed was discussed in the town.*" (It is also telling that, though the act was committed in a juridically public place, the prosecutor preferred to discover a cause of "public scandal" in it—indicating again that the judicial sense of what is "public" space remains vague.) Cf. the appeals court decision in the case of Mariana Cetiner, below. In another case, a pre-trial detention mandate from 1994 shows a prosecutor declaring that the suspect, "through threats, entered into unnatural sexual relations with G.C. [a minor], *provoking public scandal*"—although the qualification may come because the prosecutor has marked the case as Article 200, paragraph 1, instead of paragraph 2, which refers to homosexual relations with minors (Dosar no. 7351/1994, judecatoria Iasi). a curious indifference exists on the part of many law-enforcement officials to the fact that Article 200 is divided into different paragraphs with different meanings.

d) in an assembly or meeting of two or more persons, with the exception of meetings which can be considered of a family character, due to the relations between the persons participating;
e) in any way which the perpetrator is aware is likely to come to the knowledge of the public.

This definition has remained unchanged from the 1968 penal code. The code itself has no corresponding legal definition of privacy; it may indeed be questioned whether "privacy" in the sense of a zone of personal autonomy exists in the Romanian language.[93] The description offered few significant restrictions on police or judicial incursions given the society of surveillance in which it was written.[94] Letter (c), for example, could conceivably be interpreted to render many acts committed in a dwelling-place "public." Even the notion of "accessible to the public" could be problematic: Ministry of Justice officials were unable to say whether it would include a hotel room.[95]

---

[93] a term that would cover both *bodily autonomy* and a *sphere devoted to intimate relations* certainly does not exist. *Particular* carries a strong sense of owned personal property; *privat* is generally applied to private businesses or clubs. (Both terms are used as such in the penal code, and indeed the development of terminology to express private property was a significant post-Revolutionary legal concern.) The latter term occurs, in a sense probably still inflected with connotations of property, in Article 26 of the 1991 Constitution, which protects "intimate, family, and private life," as well as "the right [of a physical person] to dispose of his/her self, if it does not interfere with the rights and liberties of others, public order, or good morals." This, the strongest statement on privacy rights in Romanian law, does not address a persisting disequilibrium: that the penal code defines "public" in terms of *spaces,* while the Constitution identifies privacy more vaguely as consisting of "intimate, family, and private" *spheres.*

[94] It was of course not meant to offer such restrictions: the definition was necessitated by the fact that "commission in public" was an aggravating circumstance in a number of crimes, including theft (Article 209) and robbery (Article 211), and was a condition for slander (Article 206). The notion of limiting the definition of the public against a purely theoretical private sphere would have been meaningless in 1968.

[95] Interview with Iacovescu, Lazarescu, and Moldovan, June 1997. Interestingly, Law 61/1991 deals in parallel articles with the crime of solicitation for prostitution when committed in "parks and streets" and when committed in "hotels, motels, campgrounds, bars, restaurants, clubs, pensions, discotheques"—indicating the latter places all have an ambiguously but at least partly public status.

For gays and lesbians, however, the very existence of the "public scandal" language in paragraph 1 of Article 200 effectively renders moot the entire distinction between "private" and "public" acts. It establishes that, for a reviled minority, acts committed in what are *legally* private spaces have no defense against becoming, through no fault of their actors, objects of public concern. The language deprives gays and lesbians of equal access to privacy: a consequence compounded by the unclear definitions of privacy offered by, or implicit in, the laws, and—in overwhelming degree—by the actual transparency of supposedly "intimate" life to surveillance over four decades in Romania. Under such circumstances, for gays and lesbians, privacy becomes a scarce and chance commodity, to be captured where one can.

Beyond this, though, the new Article 200's criminalization of homosexual acts "committed in public" is clearly discriminatory. *There is no corresponding provision of the penal code which criminalizes, or even mentions, heterosexual acts committed in public.*

Human Rights Watch and IGLHRC asked repeatedly how heterosexual relations acts committed in public would be punished. Deputy Gheorghe Stancov said, "During the debates I drew the attention of other MPs to cases of heterosexuals who were caught in the act. I cited the example of a man and woman caught having sex in a park who were lightly fined. This was discrimination."[96]

Only two laws, it appears, could be applied to heterosexual sex in public. In Article 321, "a person who, in public, commits deeds or gestures, proffers words or expressions, or makes any other manifestation which tends to offend good morals or to produce public scandal" is punished with three months to two years' imprisonment—far less than Article 200, paragraph 1 provides—or a fine. Stancov also argues that the "public scandal" language common to the two laws would be invoked unequally, and limits this law's possible application to heterosexuals:

> If you see a heterosexual couple behaving in a way that suggests they have sexual relations, no one is scandalized enough to bring Article 321 to bear: it is normal sexuality, if it attracts attention it is only because we Romanians still feel a little embarrassed about publicizing such intimacies. But if two men even hug or hold hands in public, it certainly creates a scandal under Article 200. And then if it is found

---

[96] Interview with Stancov, June 1997. Some officials reacted with disbelief, probably indicating that such offenses are simply overlooked. Captain Cojocaru , "I have never seen such a case in my life, and I cannot imagine that it happens."

> they are a couple, or that they have indeed had sexual relations, they would be prosecuted.[97]

Several officials stated they would never use Article 321 to penalize heterosexual acts.[98] Captain Cojacaru of the Brasov police said the maximum punishment he could conceive would be under Law 61/1991, passed after the Revolution to regulate public behavior without filling the overcrowded jails. It imposes fines on an extensive series of violations, including "engaging in public in obscene or injurious deeds, acts, or gestures . . . which disturb the public order and peace, or which provoke the indignation of citizens."[99]

---

[97] Interview with Stancov, June 1997.

[98] Including prosecutors in Iasi, and Captain Cojocaru in Brasov. Under Ceausescu the law was titled "Hooliganism" and was a catch-all for any form of anti-social behavior the state wished to discourage.

[99] No one asked by Human Rights Watch and IGLHRC mentioned Article 201—punishing "acts of sexual perversion which cause public scandal"—as one that could be applied against heterosexual public sex, and it seems unlikely that it would be.

That said, "sexual perversion" is another elastic term, defined in the article as any "unnatural act in connection with sexual life" not covered in Article 200. The way the article is employed in practice illustrates the irrational vagueness still clouding the criminalization of sexual offenses in Romania. It is sometimes used against consensual homosexual acts—particularly against oral sex between men; apparently the understood distinction is that anal sex, imitating as it does penetrative heterosexual sex, is a "sexual relation," whereas oral sex is merely a "sexual perversion." However, this is not a universal understanding; sometimes oral sex slips back under Article 200, and sometimes anal sex is described as "sexual perversion," depending on the whims of police, prosecutor, or judge. In one characteristic case, in which the suspect was accused of both anal and oral sex, the prosecutor's indictment first charged him solely under Article 201; the final sentence, though, moved his case back entirely under Article 200. (Rechizitoriu 172/P/1995 and sentinta penala 25/1996, judecatoria Chisinau Cris.)

In practice, it would appear that only paragraphs 2 and 3 of Article 201 are enforced against heterosexuals—and here a more serious discrepancy appears: those paragraphs deal with "sexual perversion" when forced, or committed against a minor. Essentially, *rape, real or statutory, in Romanian law means vaginal intercourse* and is punished under Article 197; *other forms of forced sexual acts between a man and a woman fall under 201*—which is now the main use of that law. There, the punishment is lighter in a number of ways; in particular, the punishment for performing oral sex on a minor is two to seven years, while raping a minor carries ten to twenty; and Article 201 has no provision for the participation of more than one person (which boosts the penalty to five to fifteen years under Article 197).

Still, it is questionable whether heterosexual sex would provoke sufficient indignation to jumpstart the law—any law—into action. Asked about these discriminatory punishments, Deputy Vasile Lupu explained, "in the conception of the Romanian people, homosexual relations are abnormal and must be treated differently." One prosecutor was more direct, shouting: "All sexual relations are not equal. It is absolute craziness to expect there to be the same law for normal people and for *curisti!*"[100]

Recent Cases Under Article 200, Paragraph 1

Although the new language of Article 200, paragraph 1 came into force only in late 1996, it was clear from the time of the Constitutional Court's ruling in mid-1994 that, in order to stick, convictions should be framed so as to fall under the rubrics of "public scandal" or "committed in public."[101] It is also clear that arrests

---

Two separate cases of gang rape (sentinta penala 179/1996, judecatoria Galati; and sentinta penala 1948/1995, judecatoria Tirgu Jiu) show that participants who forced oral sex on the victim received significantly lighter sentences than those who committed (or, in the second case, merely *attempted* to commit) what one indictment calls "sexual relations with the victim by the normal means." Moreover, the language of 201 means that forced oral sex must "produce public scandal" before it can be punished! In one case where a man abducted and raped a six-year-old girl, a court must thus go out of its way to find that "his act of kissing the minor in the pubic area" produced public scandal "inasmuch as it was overheard by the witnesses in the case" (Curtea de Apel, Constanta, decizia no. 15, February 22, 1995). These absurd dispositions indicate again that a thorough rethinking of, and purging of equivocations from, the laws on sexual offenses is long overdue.

[100] Interview by Scott Long and Bogdan Voicu with criminal prosecutor Ioan Ciofu, Iasi, June 1997. An approximate translation of the term would be "buttfuckers."

[101] In a system where judicial review is a novel concept, the exact weight of the court's decision is debatable. On one hand, a May 24, 1995 letter to Amnesty International from Lieutenant General Ion Pitulescu, of the Romanian Ministry of the Interior, stated that 113 prosecutions against homosexuals during 1994 and early 1995 were undertaken "only when their acts resulted in public scandal, as specified by the Romanian penal code"—this referring to a period mainly falling *before* the court's decision was published in *Monitorul Official*, on 25 January 1995, and thus reflecting a remarkably prophetic expression of obedience. ("Romania: Amnesty International Refutes Allegations of Inaccuracy," AI Index: Eur 3911/95.) On the other hand, Captain Cojocaru of the Brasov police told Human Rights Watch and IGLHRC in July 1997 that, the court's decision was—from the perspective of the police—only a "recommendation"; parliament alone could enact decisions with the force of law.

and convictions have continued.[102] Examples of prosecutions since the Constitutional Court decision indicate a persistent difficulty in defining as "public" the space in which an act was committed—leading prosecutors to *prefer* trying cases under "public scandal," as an easier point to prove; and a discriminatory and often brutal crackdown on any expressions of homosexual desire.

The Case of Gheorghe Murariu, Constantin Pirvu, and Mircea Rusu

In May 1997 in Constanta, three homeless people—including a sixteen- and a seventeen-year-old boy—were arrested under Article 200 for sexual relations practiced in a cabin where they were living. The case displays an unrestrained use of Article 200 against populations which law enforcement officials consider undesirable—in this case, *copii ai strazii* or "street children," and other vagabonds.[103]

Human Rights Watch and IGLHRC spoke to the prosecutor in the case, Mariana Vutcovici, who alleged that Gheorghe Murariu, born in 1958, had been a "passive homosexual" since he was fourteen. A veteran of orphanages and correctional schools, he was released from jail in 1996 after serving a term for theft. From then he lived on the streets, from town to town.

Behind the Teatro Fantasio in Constanta, he discovered a row of deserted storage cabins, metal booths with doors, surrounded by a high concrete fence. In May 1997 he moved into one.[104]The cabin next to Murariu's was occupied by a group of *copii ai strazii* of varying ages. According to the prosecutor, one of them, Constantin Pirvu, sixteen, approached Murariu and invited him to have sex. They did this twice in Murariu's cabin, while—Vutcovicii claims—the other children spied through a hole in the cabin wall.

---

[102] General Paun of the IGP told Human Rights Watch and IGLHRC that three new prosecutions had been undertaken under Article 200, paragraph 1 between January and May, 1997. Human Rights Watch and IGLHRC themselves are aware of four. It is likely that there have been still others.

[103] This account is based on interviews by Vera Campeanu and Scott Long with the prosecutor and the accused, in June 1997. a short account of the arrests, based on information released by the police during the investigation, appeared in a national newspaper: Lizeta Anton, "Doi minori si un adult faceau sex oral," *Evenimentul zilei,* May 30, 1997.

[104] Under arrest, Murariu confessed that he had sex with another homeless man living there: the prosecutor told Human Rights Watch and IGLHRC that investigators were looking for this person as an additional suspect, but that Murariu had refused to give his name.

On May 26, 1997, in the same place, Murariu also had sex with Mircea Rusu, seventeen, whom the prosecutor identified as another "street child." They were caught in the act by two civil guards, who took all three of them to the police.

Murariu was charged Article 200 paragraph 2, for sexual relations with minors. However, because the minors acted "with free will and under no constraint," the prosecutor also charged them under paragraph 1. The machinery of the law was scrupulously attentive: Pirvu was charged on two counts, having had sex with Murariu twice; moreover, because he allegedly stood guard outside the cabin, he made himself an accessory to Murariu's and Rusu's crime. "For all that," the prosecutor said, "he will get six years, and perhaps serve all of it."[105]

In the indictment and in an interview with Human Rights Watch and IGLHRC, the prosecutor identified the act not as "committed in public" but as "causing public scandal." Significantly, she preferred not to enter into the legal question of whether a closed cabin was "public" under Article 152, instead explaining that the sexual acts either were seen by or became known to the other street children," who were "scandalized by them."

In June 1997, Human Rights Watch and IGLHRC were able to speak to the three accused separately in the Constanta lockup, where they had been held since their arrest. The interviews were supervised by Major Minea, the head of the lockup, who interrupted repeatedly, refused to allow certain questions, and bullied the two minors about their replies. "You cannot treat these children as if they are innocent," he said. "You are not allowed to encourage them. If they were set free, they would go back to the same cabin and do the same things."

Constantin Pirvu and Mircea Rusu were crying throughout the interviews. Constantin said he had run away from his family only three weeks before his arrest. Mircea, despite the prosecutor's statements, was not a "street child." He lived with his parents, knew Constantin and his family who had been their neighbors, and had been visiting the cabins because he ran into Constantin near the theater on the night in question. His parents had not been permitted to visit him since his arrest. "I did it willingly but if I had known what it meant I wouldn't have done it," he said, crying uncontrollably.

Gheorghe Murariu was barefoot and in torn clothes. In the presence of Major Minea, he said that all three had been beaten severely after their arrest, both by the civil guards and by a major in the municipal police. He claimed to have suffered since from difficulty in breathing because of the beatings. Murariu cannot read or

[105] Interview by Vera Campeanu and Scott Long with prosecutor Mariana Vutcovici, Constanta, June 1997.

write. He said that at the municipal police station he signed three statements under threat of further beatings, but was not told what was in them.

All three are now facing trial.

The Case of Radu Vasiliu and Adrian Gabriel Presnac

In Iasi, in September 1996, two seventeen-year-old boys were arrested and charged under Article 200, paragraph 1. Police asserted they were having sexual relations in public: the two maintain they were only kissing. Both also recount how police beat them sadistically for hours. Their account reaffirms that any public expression of homosexuality can be transformed—under police pressure—into "sexual relations," and made punishable under Article 200.[106]

Radu Vasiliu and Adrian Gabriel ("Gabi") Presnac both come from extremely poor, working-class families in Iasi; Gabi was taken from his parents' custody some years ago by the state, and given to his grandmother. The two lived in the same neighborhood, and had been close friends for several years. At around 8:00 PM on the night of September 15, 1996, they found themselves drinking a bottle of wine on the grounds of a restaurant, shielded by bushes and shaded by a tree. The two boys sat there, in relative seclusion. Both insist firmly that no sexual act took place: that they were only embracing and kissing.

The doorman saw them from the terrace. As he approached, he saw them touching. Presnac remembers him shouting: "*Curisti!*" With a waiter, he dragged the two to a police car parked nearby.

The car held four policemen. The boys were stretched on the ground, searched, and asked if they had stolen anything. According to Presnac, officers kicked him twice in the stomach as he lay on the ground; when they were loaded in the car, he was slapped several times.

At the Sector 2 police station, police ordered them to write statements which officers dictated to them. Vasiliu says he "had problems" with his statement—Presnac elaborates that his friend has difficulty writing. Because he ruined two sheets of paper, policemen hit him five times with clubs in the palms of his hands.

---

[106] Representatives of IGLHRC visited Iasi in September 1996 and interviewed Radu Vasiliu and Gabriel Presnac, along with members of their family, Major Bodea of the judetean police, and Major Barlica, commandant of the municipal poilce. Human Rights Watch and IGLHRC returned in June 1997 to speak to Radu Vasiliu; Gabriel Presnac's grandmother; the lawyer for the accused, Aspasia Boia; and officials in the prosecutor's office. This account is based on those interviews.

Asked his age, Presnac responded that he was eighteen, "minus two months."[107] Police demanded that he write in the statement simply that he was eighteen—perhaps hoping to charge him as an adult for having sex with a minor. He gave his grandmother's address, but police records still showed him living with his parents:

> They said I was lying and they beat me very hard. There was a tall blond man in civilian dress who singled me out. He hit me with fists in the forehead and the back of the head. They wanted to know who else I did it with, and they beat me sadistically to get names and addresses. They kept knocking my head against a desk, till one of my teeth was knocked out and there was blood pouring from my mouth. Finally, I admitted that I had had sex with a foreign student who had left the country. Then the blond policeman took me into another room for another statement. He asked me which of us had the idea first "to do something like this." I told him that whatever we did, we both wanted to do it. He told me, "Your friend has already said you were the one who came up with the idea." He hit me in the head and struck me with his club till I added to my declaration that I had started it. They were always asking us who was the girl, who was the boy. I would tell them, "We are both boys": then they'd slap and hit me. We were like two punching bags.

Meanwhile, police were pressuring Vasiliu (the taller and stronger of the two) to write in his statement that he had raped Presnac—threatening him, "We'll beat you to death": it appears they were toying with several different frameworks for charging the boys. Vasiliu eventually produced a statement, under dictation, in which he said the two had anal sex in which Vasiliu played the active role; then had oral sex, reversing roles—all this taking place under the tree near the restaurant.

The two were handcuffed and, around 11:00 PM, taken by car to the central municipal police station. There police slapped their faces again and hit them over the shoulders. They were separated and put in cells. A policeman told Vasiliu to stand with his face to the wall of his cell, "because I'm sick of you." For the next hour, whenever the guard passed the cell, he would enter and beat Vasiliu if he noticed his head turned away from the wall. Finally the boy was allowed to lie down and sleep.

---

[107] He was born on November 16, 1978.

In the morning the two boys were fingerprinted, then returned to the lockup. Vasiliu was put with his face to the wall, while Presnac was forced to wash the floor of the three cells in the lockup and the corridor. They were then hauled to the police toilets. Vasiliu was given a chip of brick and told to scrape the filthy toilet bowls clean; his head was shoved in the bowl while it was flushed. Police urinated in the urinals; then Presnac was made to clean them with his bare hands.

In the afternoon they were taken to the hospital. Doctor Pandeli, a forensic expert, performed tests on the penis and anus of each. Presnac complained that she hurt his anus in inserting a probe. She retorted: "You like it when you stick a huge cock up your anus: it doesn't hurt then."

At the station, they were again separated: new declarations were dictated to them, recapitulating the previous ones. While Presnac wrote his, police struck him till his nose bled; one policeman kicked him again and again, calling him a "perverse whore." Finally, at about 7:00 PM, they were released.

Although they were free for the moment, the legal case still hung over them. According to Presnac's grandmother, police in the neighborhood followed and harassed him for months, till his parents "begged them to stop beating him." In December, he fled; his whereabouts are unknown. The grandmother believes he may have left the country; Vasiliu fears he has committed suicide.

The Romanian Helsinki Committee hired a lawyer for the two. The attorney told Human Rights Watch and IGLHRC that "gossip around the court" was that prosecutors were embarrassed by the case and initially wished to drop it. However, an indictment was handed down in December 1996, charging the two under both Article 200, paragraph 1 and Article 201, paragraph 1, and accusing them of having both oral and anal sex outside the restaurant.[108] In this case, too, the two are cited for producing public scandal, by scandalizing the persons who surprised them.

Their case has not yet come to trial.

The Cases of Florian Cristian Hanganu and Stefan Harabula, and of Gavril Bors and Mihai Tintila

Examples of men arrested for homosexual acts since the Constitutional Court's decision in 1994 indicate discriminatory punishment for trespasses in the public sphere. Human Rights Watch and IGLHRC stress again the statements of police and prosecutors that the following offenses, if committed by heterosexuals, would be unlikely to lead to arrest and detention, much less a prison term.

[108] Interview by Scott Long and Bogdan Voicu with Aspasia Boia, Iasi, June 1997; see also dosar nr. 5806/1996, judecatoria Iasi.

The central railway station of Iasi, like many other stations around Romania, is a meeting place for gay men: and Iasi police and prosecutors may possess a particular animus against them. In early June 1997, two men, Florin Cristian Hanganu and Stelian Harabula, were arrested for entering into sexual relations in a stall of the men's toilet in the station. According to prosecutors, the cleaning man in the toilet "heard a suspicious noise, looked in the keyhole, and caught the two."[109] He forcibly kept the two from leaving the stall while summoning the station police with his shouts.

In the presence of police and the prosecutor in the case, Human Rights Watch and IGLHRC also spoke to the two arrested men, who essentially confirmed this account. At the time Human Rights Watch and IGLHRC investigated the case, the two had been held in pre-trial detention for almost a month. Chief Prosecutor Varvescu stated that "it is not a case of human rights but a case of children," explaining that if released the two would "make proselytism" and corrupt street children living in the station. Neither of the two men has a prior record, and there is no reason to suspect them of sexual abuse of children. A case from 1996 of a French national who solicited street children in the Bucharest station was heavily publicized; this may explain the concern of the prosecutor for a population who, as the Constanta case indicates, infrequently experience any measure of solicitude on the part of the law. The prosecutor in the case, Constantin Crismaru, later remarked that he had wished to drop charges, but Prosecutor Varvescu insisted on pressing them.

Gavril Bors and Mihai Tintila were arrested under almost exactly identical circumstances in the Iasi station, almost exactly one year earlier, on June 5, 1996. Tintila's file[110] shows that a cleaning man surprised them in a stall of the station toilet and called the police. The court sentence cites the act as producing public scandal; both the cleaning man and the two police offices responding to the call were scandalized by what they found. Both men were sentenced to and year and six months' imprisonment under Article 200. Bors's sentence was suspended; Tintila, who resisted arrest, received an additional one year and three months for "offense to authority" and "outrage" (Articles 238 and 239), and was remanded to serve the longer sentence.

Interviewed in Iasi penitentiary, Tintila stated that when he and Bors had been in the stall for two or three minutes, police came, smashing the latch, and took them

---

[109] The case was reported in a small note in *Evenimentul zilei*, June 5, 1997. Human Rights Watch and IGLHRC spoke in June 1997 to Acting Chief Prosecutor Evgenia Varvescu of Iasi, as well as to Constantin Crismaru, the prosecutor in the case.

[110] Dosar penetenciar 63/1996, Iasi; sentinta penala 3759/96, judecatoria Iasi.

to the police post in the station. There a *plutionier* or junior officer insulted and slapped Tintila, who responded by running away. He was caught by a sergeant and the plutonier; after a brief altercation in which Tintila hit the two with a shopping bag, he was dragged back to the station, where he was beaten, kicked and strangled by seven or eight officers for half an hour.[111]

---

[111] Interview by Scott Long and Yves Nya Ngatchou with Mihai Tintila in Iasi penitentiary, June 1997. In a similar case documented by the Romanian Helsinki Committee, Catalin Bucur and Stefan Ciocirlan were arrested by police in Focsani on July 4, 1995. Bucur, who was seventeen, told the Committee that—while waiting for a train to take him to the orphanage where he lived—he took a walk in Focsani and, in a park in the night, met Ciocirlan. Shielded behind bushes, they masturbated. Police and public guards caught them as Bucur was zipping his fly, while Ciocirlan, fully dressed, lay on the ground. Bucur states that police immediately told one of the public guards to "go fetch three civil witnesses." The witnesses were duly produced and were duly scandalized. Although a new text of Article 200 had not yet been adopted, police evidently felt it important to meet the "public scandal" requirement—yet again indicating confusion on the part of law-enforcement officials between the two conditions imposed by the Constitutional Court. They were charged under Article 200. Interview by Ion Iacos and Manuela Stefanescu of the Romanian Helsinki Committee with Bucur in Focsani Penitentiary, 1995. The Romanian Helsinki Committee has not been able to trace the ultimate disposition of Bucur's and Ciocirlan's case.

5. FREEDOM OF EXPRESSION AND ASSOCIATION

Before 1996, the final paragraph of Article 200 punished "inciting or encouraging" a person to engage in homosexual relations, with one to five years' imprisonment. The new version passed in that year tacks on an additional restriction, subjecting "propaganda, association, or any act of proselytism" to the same punishment.

These two clauses deserve to be discussed separately. The first may originally have been directed at solicitation—simply approaching another person, or inviting someone to engage in sexual contact. As such it solidified in the 1968 code the idea only implicit in 1936's law, that the pursuit of so-called "clients"— sexual partners—by homosexuals represented a social danger.[112] However, it also overlapped—as it still does—with Article 204, which criminalized even the *attempt* to engage in sexual offenses (including Article 200). As if to foreclose all loopholes, multiple laws thus penalize the open articulation of desire.

"Inciting and Encouraging": The Case of Mariana Cetiner

In 1991, Major Catalineanu—then head of the Bucharest vice squad, and a figure of terror to many gay men—told an interviewer, "In eighteen years I never compiled a file on lesbians. . . . I have never come across such a case, none ever landed on our desks."[113] Social and cultural barriers to women's voicing lesbian desire were severe—sufficiently so that the law rarely had to act. But the law was ready.

Mariana Cetiner, born in 1957, was abandoned by her mother and grew up in an orphanage. A sportswoman, at twelve she was transferred to a special school for athletes. Ultimately she married a Turkish citizen, and lived in Istanbul for a time.

In 1994-95, she played in a handball team in the Netherlands. In August 1995 she returned to Romania, settling in the Transylvanian city of Alba Iulia. She moved into an apartment with a married woman, Elena Mihailescu; another woman who lived there, Adina Vana, "collaborated in commercial business" with Cetiner, according to the indictment. (Cetiner apparently lent her 4000 DM—about $3000.)

---

[112] The only remotely equivalent provision covering heterosexuals is again in Law 61/1991, paragraph 6—which punishes (with a fine) solicitation for prostitution.

[113] Interview with Catalineanu by Camelia Doru, "Si politistii sint oameni . . ." *Opinia medicala,* no. 21/1991, August 29-September 14, 1991.

For asking Adina Vana to have sex with her, Mariana Cetiner would be sentenced to three years in prison. Her penal file[114] contains her indictment, the statements of the two "victims" who shared the apartment with her, and statements by witnesses. The indictment claims:

> Due to limited space, the suspect and the victim Adina Vana were forced to sleep in the same room on several occasions, until one night when Mariana Cetiner began to reveal to the victim aspects of her intimate life, explaining at last that she was a lesbian and had had intimate relations with women in Alba Iulia, giving the names of some of these persons. At the same time she expressed the wish to enter into these relations together; letting it be known that she loved the victim and could offer a different sexual satisfaction, proposing even that they could marry in Holland, the law of which tolerates unnatural marriages. The victim refused this proposal categorically, explaining that she was a normal woman from the sexual point of view and did not approve of those who practiced homosexual relations.

The requests continued, however—fifteen or twenty times, according to Vana. Although Article 200 does not require that "incitement or encouragement" provoke a public scandal, the indictment is at pains to establish that Cetiner's behavior did so. One night events "achieved unnatural intensity and came to the knowledge of other persons," when, on an overnight trip the three women took to the mountains, the suspect experienced an "exaggerated growth of her abnormal sexual impulses," and left the room violently, throwing glasses.

Cetiner moved out of the apartment; and soon after, Elena Mihailescu, on behalf of the victim Vana, reported Cetiner to the police. It appears she carried evidence with her: the indictment notes,

> to prove her sentiments of love, the suspect had offered the victim her own photographs, on which she inscribed a text with contents suggestive of her intentions. On another occasion, believing it insufficient to convince the victim through verbal dialogue, she wrote "love letters" which took part in the erotic "game" of being a couple.

---

[114] Dosar no. 3223/1996, judecatoria Alba, rechizitoriu no. 2516/P/1995. Copies of these documents are on file with Human Rights Watch and IGLHRC.

One morning, Cetiner appeared at the two women's door, bringing a male witness. According to this man, there was an argument: Cetiner refused to leave the apartment. Mihailescu went to a neighbor's phone to call police; while she was gone, Cetiner departed. The same day, Cetiner was arrested under the charges of Article 200, "the last paragraph,"[115] and for violation of a domicile (for remaining in Mihailescu's apartment).

Police also sought witnesses to confirm Cetiner's lesbian behavior. One writes,

> I met Mariana Cetiner [at a party] and because I understood from the hostess that this Mariana was lesbi [sic], I showed curiosity about it, what this thing meant and whether in truth the woman in question was lesbi. So, at a given moment, profiting from her state of drunkenness, I asked her directly "whether or not she was lesbian." She responded, "Yes, I am" . . .

Cetiner's own statement to police is brief. She denies "inciting or encouraging" Vana, saying she had lent Vana money and wanted it back.

She was subjected to a number of psychiatric examinations, and was not even indicted until she had spent seven months in jail. Neither judge nor prosecutors questioned the comparative weight of the two charges against her: she was sentenced to three years under Article 200, "last paragraph," and to only six months for violation of domicile.[116]

Cetiner appealed. Her appeal was granted—under a convoluted argument.[117] Although all parties had denied that any sexual contact had taken place, the appeals tribunal, without explanation, decided that "the suspect had entered into such a relation with Adina Vana after proposing it."[118]

---

[115] Prosecutors did not specify the number, knowing that what was then paragraph 4 of Article 200 would become paragraph 5 if the version under debate passed—which seemed likely to happen before a trial.

[116] Sentinta penala no. 715/1996, jud. Alba; the two sentences were combined for a total of three years.

[117] Decizia penala no. 12/a/1997, January 13, 1997, Tribunalul Alba. Elena Mihailescu had in the meantime withdrawn her complaint against Cetiner for violation of domicile.

[118] In her original statement to police, Vana had been justifiably anxious to stress that her relations with Cetiner were not sexual—lest she be arrested as well: however, she records that "In the time I stayed with the Mihailescu family I slept with [Cetiner] at most two or

The presumption of a sexual act created a new legal situation. "Actions of inciting and encouraging [are] absorbed in the contents of the infractions specified in Article 200, paragraph 1": instead of paragraph 5, the court contended the act fell under the first paragraph. However, the tribunal then examined the question of public scandal, finding that "none of the special conditions of incriminalization are assembled here." While "between the accused and the victim Adina Vana many scandals did take place, these occurred because Adina Vana refused to return twenty million lei" which the accused had lent her—not because of the supposed sexual relationship. By the court's tangled reasoning, Cetiner should not have been charged under paragraph 1, either. In January 1997, after serving fourteen months, Cetiner was—briefly— freed from prison.

Prosecutors then filed a further appeal, objecting that the tribunal had misjudged the relations between the two women, as well as misunderstood the nature of public scandal. This argument was accepted by the highest local appeals court in May 1997.[119] It moved the case back under the "last paragraph" of 200, thus exonerating Adina Vana of having succumbed to Cetiner's urgings; it found that while there had been a "dispute referring to a financial matter," the main dispute had involved intimate relations, and "with certainty the condition of public scandal was fulfilled."[120] Mariana Cetiner was arrested again ten days later and began serving the remainder of her sentence.

Human Rights Watch and IGLHRC asked the chief prosecutor of Alba Iulia whether "inciting or encouraging" a person of the *opposite* sex to sexual relations would initiate a criminal case. He seemed surprised by the question. "It is not

---

three nights but since we were in the presence of Mrs. Mihailescu she did nothing more than kiss me on the neck, the face, and the back, caress me on the breasts, and other gestures of the same sort. Mrs. Mihailescu also slept in the same room." The tribunal may well have found that these gestures constituted "sexual relations" between women—particularly given the continuing uncertainty, in Romanian law, surrounding exactly how "sexual relations" are to be defined.

[119] Dosar nr. 731/1997, decizia penala no. 166/1997, Curtea de Apel Alba Iulia, May 6, 1997.

[120] In the process implicitly accepting the argument, nowhere made before, that paragraph 5—which does not mention public scandal—is still qualified by it; indicating at least a somewhat cavalier indifference to precision.

punishable by any means," he said. Cetiner's lesbianism he called "the hobby of a woman of dubious morality."[121]

Human Rights Watch and IGLHRC also visited Mariana Cetiner in Tirgsor penitentiary. The conversation was supervised, by two guards who seemed determined to threaten Cetiner. She was able to communicate briefly in English, before guards stopped her. She said an officer had beaten her the day before, because she tried to file a complaint: "He handcuffed me and pulled me out of my cell by the hair. I have much to say but it is forbidden. When you leave, I will have big problems." When transferred from Aiud penitentiary in May, she said, she had spent four days on a train without food or water. "I grew up in an orphanage, that was awful, but to end up here is worse."

Cetiner had a large bruise on her right thigh, and her knee was bandaged. She attempted to show another bruise, on her side, but was afraid in the guards' presence. In Romanian, before the guards, she had little to say. She seemed confused, and repeated she had been framed because Adina Vana refused to repay a twenty million lei loan.[122]

Human Rights Watch and IGLHRC believe that Mariana Cetiner has been physically abused in prison, and that her sexual orientation has been a factor in this abuse. Dr. Maria Anghel of the prison clinic acknowledged, "I don't try to defend the guards, but you must see she is a difficult person, perverse, not at all normal. After fourteen hours of working hard, the means a guard uses to get such a person down to quiet down may not always be the most gentle."[123]

"Propaganda, Association, or Any Form of Proselytism"

Human Rights Watch and IGLHRC asked a number of officials what the new language in paragraph 5 prohibits. "Public scandal" has attracted the bulk of international attention: these interviews suggest that paragraph 5 comprises still more serious threats to basic freedoms of expression and assembly.

---

[121] Interview by Scott Long and Bogdan Voicu with Luha, July 1997.

[122] Interview by Scott Long and Bogdan Voicu with Mariana Cetiner, Tirgsor Penitenciary, July 1997.

[123] Interview by Long and Voicu with Maria Anghel, Tirgsor penitentiary, July 1997. Most guards and staff at Tirgsor are men. Members of the mission were able to speak briefly to inmates who described how—during a hunger strike throughout the prison system in the spring—guards entered the recidivists' ward and beat the women in their beds. When the strike broke, the strikers were taken outside and made to crawl face down across a field while guards beat them.

Asked, for instance, about the legality of commercial gathering places for gays or lesbians, General Paun of the General Inspectorate of Police illuminated exactly how homosexuals appear as a group to law-enforcement officials:

> Any bar or office where homosexuals meet would be illegal under paragraph 5, even if no sexual activity is going to take place there. If a a bar were to declare this its purpose, the court would not grant a license: the law punishes any offense to public morals. *That is why bordellos are banned: and this case would correspond exactly to the sanctions against organized prostitution.* (Emphasis added)[124]

Ana Iacovescu of the Ministry of Justice was more hopeful: "My answer is, this may be allowed with time. We have made steps in defending rights of this minority, but we may be pressing too far, too fast." Colonel Moldovan added: "Civil society is not ready for this."[125]

Senator Ion Vasile said a private commercial establishment "would be absolutely illegal," even if no sexual activity took place there. And Deputy Vasile Lupu argued that if the establishment served people who were not gay as well as people who were, it could be cited for proselytism.

Similar responses came to questions about gay and lesbian organizations. Law 21/1924 provides that, for an organization to be legally registered, a local court, local prosecutor, and the Ministry closest to its stated scope of activities must investigate whether its statutes are compatible with existing legislation. Asked if the Ministry of Justice would approve a gay and lesbian rights organization, Ana Iacovescu wondered "whether we have reached the stage when we could accept an organization of homosexuals having legal status. I do not think so." Senator Vasile said, "I can hardly believe that they could obtain legal status. They are associations. Paragraph 5 makes associations illegal."[126]

Magazines, publications, and public events are likewise banned. According to Deputy Emil Popescu, "If a lesbian were to go out in the streets dressed to protest, it is not certain she would get away alive. This law exists to protect her from doing so."[127]

---

[124] Interview by Campeanu and Long with Gen. Paun, June 1997.

[125] Interview by Campeanu and Long with Iacovescu, June 1997.

[126] Interview by Campeanu and Long with Sen. Vasile, June 1997.

[127] Interview by Campeanu and Long with Deputy Popescu, June 1997.

One of the few attempts to test the tolerance of police and prosecutors came in 1994, when an activist organized a cultural festival in Bucharest, "Together Against Homophobia and AIDS." Several Scandinavian artists and musicians agreed to perform. On its opening day—July 15, the same day on which the Supreme Court ruled that homosexual acts could be penalized "if they cause public scandal"—the director of the host theater canceled all performances, saying he had not known "the sexual inclinations of the performers and organizers."[128]

Organizers managed to reschedule the events for the next night at a *casa de cultura,* or municipal cultural center, in the capital. The director of the cultural house later told the press that "all of Bucharest immediately jumped on my head, from the mayor on down". He claimed he had received a call from a "high political personality" saying that if the performances took place, "in twenty-four hours the casa de cultura would be closed or demolished."

When performers and audience arrived on the night of July 16, they found the casa de cultura ringed by police, all armed and with dogs, barring entry. On order of the mayor of Sector 4 in Bucharest, "to protect public morals," the festival was shut down.[129]

There has never been an openly gay bar in Romania.[130] However, in the summer of 1996, an outdoor cafe owned by a gay man opened in a secluded part of Herastrau Park in Bucharest. Many gays frequented it. One night in November, it was raided by five men who assaulted the customers and destroyed windows, furniture, and equipment. Police at a nearby station were alerted; they refused to intervene and reportedly laughed at the possibility of physical danger to

---

[128] Bogdan Tiberiu Iacob, "Teatrul 'Ion Creanga' a anuntat ca nu va mai permite desfasurarea pe scene sa a Festivalului 'Gay & Lesbian,'" *Tineretul liber,* July 15, 1994.

[129] Cristina Sofronie and Bogdan Iacob, "Artistii europeani au facut cale intoarsa . . ." *Tineretul liber,* July 18, 1994; Catalina Ciutac, "Festivalul International al Homosexualilor si Lesbienilor," *Evenimentul zilei*, July 18, 1994; Eric Kubista, press release from *Kom Ut,* Sweden, July 20, 1994.

[130] Gays in Bucharest usually informally colonize a few bars or cafes near the main cruising area, the Opera Park. Owners who realize what is happening often try to drive them out: representatives of Human Rights Watch and IGLHRC witnessed gay men refused service and harassed at a terrace near the Opera Park over several nights in June 1997.

customers.[131] The bar shut down not long after. Its owner, interviewed by Human Rights Watch and IGLHRC, said, "There cannot be an openly gay bar here, and there cannot be a bar that is just for gays."[132]

Similarly, there has never been a legally registered gay/lesbian NGO in Romania, and no group has dared to test the limits. [133] ACCEPT, a human-rights group of gays, lesbians, and their supporters, sought legal registration in 1996. A lawyer advised them that, even under the old version of Article 200, if their registration papers explicitly mentioned "sexual minorities" or homosexuality, both the Ministry of Justice and the court would see it as "an encouragement of crimes." [134] All such references were deleted, and ACCEPT registered as a general human-rights organization in October 1996.

In early 1997, the Concordia Foundation—a nonprofit cultural foundation—applied for registration to the Municipal Court of Bucharest. Its statutes committed it to defend "cultural communities (ethnic, linguistic, religious) in Romania," and to "combat intolerance in all its forms (homophobia, xenophobia, racism.)" The court decided in their favor, but the prosecutor's office appealed, arguing that the term "cultural community" was unclear and that the forms of intolerance listed were inappropriate. Orally, he instructed the group to remove "homophobia" from the statutes.[135]

---

[131] Interview by Scott Long with Daniel Iorga, July 1997.

[132] Interview by Scott Long with "Razvan," June 1997.

[133] Surveillance of gay and lesbian circles, and any more formal groups that arise, is probably extensive—as a case in Baia-Mare, in the next chapter, indicates. A Cluj student, who in 1993 was asked (in a private residence) to translate materials that a fledgling gay organization in Bucharest could distribute, was summoned within hours by the local branch of the SRI (the former Securitate or Ceausescu-era secret police); he was told that he was "cooperating with an alliance of homosexuals and Hungarians who want to destroy the Romanian state." Interview by Scott Long with Horatiu R., March 1993.

[134] Interviews by Scott Long with Adrian Coman and Ion Iacos, June 1997.

[135] Interview by Yves Nya Ngatchou with Florin Buhuceanu of Fundatia Concordia, July 1997.

6. DISCRIMINATION IN DEFINING THE "AGE OF CONSENT"

Since homosexuality has at best been incompletely decriminalized in Romania, one cannot properly speak of an "age of consent" for homosexual acts. However, paragraph 2 of Article 200—which punishes "the act of an adult having sexual relations with a minor of the same sex" with two to seven years' imprisonment "and denial of certain rights"—is discriminatory in two ways.[136]

Both the *description of* and the *punishment for* the act are inequable. A minor in Romanian law is any person under eighteen. However, the corresponding provision covering heterosexual acts, Article 198—"sexual relations with a minor girl"—punishes only "sexual relations with a person of the feminine sex *under the age of fourteen*". The penalty, one to five years in prison, is substantially smaller.[137]

Nicula Stelian's case illustrates concretely what these distinctions can mean. Stelian was eighteen when arrested in his village in southeastern Romania. A young man named Nicusor T., whom he described as "effeminate," had shown some interest in him in the past, always trying to spend time with him. Nicusor T. was seventeen, one year behind Stelian in school.

In August 1993, Stelian told IGLHRC representatives, the two left a dance in the village, both a little drunk. They went into the hay in a yard behind a house; Stelian opened his pants and they had oral sex. The incident was never repeated.

In the next month, however—three or four weeks later—Stelian was arrested by the police. He believes that Nicusor T. had confessed to his mother, who had complained to the police.

Stelian was taken to the village police post and severely beaten. Two police officers, calling him a "pederast," hit him on the chest with their fists, and kicked him on the legs repeatedly. He showed IGLHRC representatives scars on his shins

---

[136] Under Article 200 in its 1968 version, paragraph 2 also included homosexual rape, imposing the same punishment of two to seven years—with the resultant and surely unintended peculiarity that homosexual rape was punished more lightly than heterosexual rape (liable to three to ten years' imprisonment under Article 197). This has now been corrected; in a separate paragraph 3, homosexual rape receives three to ten years.

However, "denial of certain rights" was added as a punishment in 1996 to paragraphs 2-4 of Article 200. As specified in Article 64 of the penal code, this can include the denial, after a penal sentence has been served, of the right to vote, the right to occupy a government post, the right to practice certain other occupations, and parental rights. In a further instance of discrimination, these punishments cannot be imposed when the corresponding acts are committed in a heterosexual context (as provided in Article 197 and 198).

[137] Romanian law provides no age of consent for males in a heterosexual relationship.

which he said were from the beatings: after several months, there were still perceptible indentations on his flesh. The beatings continued for several hours, till he wrote down the statements they dictated for him.

He was released, but arrested again in October, and spent thirty days in pre-trial detention. Stelian says that when he met the prosecutor, the latter told his assistant to write down Article 200, paragraph 1 in the arrest warrant. The assistant said, "No, paragraph 2—we only write paragraph 2 now." The slight difference in his age and Nicusor's enabled the crucial change.

Stelian remembers the judge at the trial saying that "this case should not justify imprisonment": he seemed to consider granting a suspended sentence. The prosecutor in arguments stressed that Stelian had engaged in sexual relations with a minor. He was sentenced to three years under Article 200, paragraph 2.[138]

[138] Dosar no. 3256/1993, judecatoria Urziceni; interview by Scott Long and Yves Nya Ngatchou with Nicula Stelian in Poarta Alba penitentiary, January 1995.

7. ABUSES BY POLICE AND OTHER OFFICIALS

Surveillance, Blackmail, Control

Captain Cojocaru of the Brasov police assured Human RIghts Watch and IGLHRC, "We do not monitor gay meeting places. No one in Brasov keeps files on homosexuals; we have no undercover police." General Paun of the General Inspectorate of Police affirmed, "The police do not target homosexuals—we target situations where criminal actions are committed by homosexuals," adding that the Inspectorate department investigating "infractions of sexual life" was shut down after 1990, "just like the department that dealt with Gypsies."[139]

This is an overstatement: municipal and county police departments retain "morals" divisions under various names, most with a special brief to monitor homosexuals. Major Catalineanu, head of the vice squad in the Bucharest municipal police, told an interviewer in 1991 that his "*varianta*" department dealt with "forgery, fraud, prostitution and pandering, juvenile delinquency, and homosexuality."[140]

There is, indeed, ample evidence that police regard homosexuals as a special and suspect class, and justify surveillance by the argument that they are more disposed to crime. The notion of "pathological homosexual jealousy" frequently recurs. A recently published *Dictionary of Useful Legal Terms*, co-authored by the head of the General Inspectorate of Police, contains a special entry on "homosexuality" (although the term itself nowhere occurs in legislation), characterizing it by "misogyny in men, androphobia in women, and jealousy toward the partner of the same sex."[141] General Paun observed, "There are many cases of homosexual murders, terribly vicious, particularly partners in a couple." Captain Cojocaru said, "Homosexuals are very jealous: the moment when a partner is betrayed, murder can easily result." And—also in Brasov—Maj. Stefan Bancila, chief of the homicide division of the county police, undermined Captain Cojocaru's

---

[139] It would be hard to contend that eliminating a division specifically targeting Roma has significantly mitigated the tendency throughout law enforcement in Romania toward automatic presumption of their guilt.

[140] Interview by Doru, "Si politistii sint oameni . . ." *Opinia medicala*, 1991.

[141] Pitulescu et. al, p. 209. The entire article makes an implicit case for full criminalization of homosexuality, arguing that "Specialists sustain that homosexuality falls under the category of perversions in which are comprised pedophilia, zoophilia, necrophilia, etc. . . . In many countries, homosexuality is forbidden by law because it produces disturbances in adaptation and familial and social integration."

earlier assurances, telling IGLHRC that gay cruising areas "are breeding places of crime and murder, and of course we have informants there all the time."[142]

One newspaper describes Col. Tudor Butoi, a psychologist in the Bucharest Municipal Police, as "perhaps the number one specialist in Romania on homosexual behavior." This expert often regales the press with the horrors of homosexuality:

> Murders among homosexuals have distinctive features. By contrast with crimes committed suddenly and spontaneously . . . the homosexual killer operates with premeditation, surprising the victim (often in a home they share), acting with a ferocity typically moved by savage jealousy . . . The danger does not disappear at all in the case of homosexual couples. Their jealousy is pathological. Stable couples are difficult to form. Their relations are as a rule occasional and the partners are capricious and unstable. When they attain a lasting relationship, the egoistic feeling of possession is exacerbated. Life in a homosexual couple is far from easy. For a normal man, it is excruciating torture to enter the dwelling of such a pair. In general it is a horrible pit, stinking with filth. Aging homosexuals suffer from fecal incontinence. Due to anal relations, over time, the sphincter gives way. . . .The durability of couples is maintained through gifts, money, food, orgies. Not uncommonly, the homosexual also blackmails the partner, in order not to lose him, or commits murder from jealousy. . . . To be lenient to homosexuality would be a criminal experiment.[143]

"I don't believe homosexuality is acquired by heredity," Butoi told another reporter. "The genesis of this phenomenon is in adults perverting children. . . . Homosexuality, like prostitution, is the factor which germinates theft, vagabondage, and crime." [144] Such malign stereotypes are evidently rampant among police.

---

[142] Interview by Daniel Iorga and Ioana Stancel with Maj. Stefan Bancila, July 1997.

[143] Miruna Munteanu, "Crimele comis de homosexuali," *Zeghea,* August 13-19, 1996.

[144] Zaschievici and Barbii, "Crimele oribile comis in ultimul timp . . ." *Libertatea,* November 9, 1996.

Major Catalineanu told an interviewer, "Some of the police officers would like to shoot homosexuals."[145]

Catalineanu was a well-known figure to gay men in Bucharest for years. One who received asylum in the Netherlands remembers him as heading "teams of informers and policemen who beat up, chase, and even seduce homosexuals.[146]

Bogdan Dumitrescu is a gay man who has a long history with the Bucharest police, as a suspect and as an unwilling source of information. He reports that:

> The police have always kept files on homosexuals. They are always interested in people in high positions, and it was those they mostly asked me about. But if they ever asked me about people I knew from the Opera Park, I refused to tell them.
>
> Catalineanu looked after people who informed for him. There was a prosecutor in Sector 5 in Bucharest who in 1991 was blackmailing a number of gays with threats of criminal cases. He came to my home, trying to be tough, threatening to arrest me, trying to get names from me I people I had had sexual relations with. I went to Catalineanu, and he made certain that nothing happened. The prosecutor picked up some gay students at the university in the middle of an examination. Catelineanu got them out of jail, because they had worked for him.
>
> In 1993, Catalineanu finally was promoted to the antiterrorism squad. He destroyed the files on homosexuals before leaving, so that now, when a new crime involving homosexuals happens, only he will have the information, at his disposal in his head. After 1990 policemen received a 20,000 lei bonus [$200 in 1990] for each crime they solved: Catalineanu wants that money for himself. His successors have to come to Catalineanu for information; Catalineanu gives it only if he gets the bonus.

---

[145] Doru, "Si politistii sint oameni . . ."

[146] Cristian Constantin, quoted in Jolande van der Graaf, "Roemenie jaagt op homoseksuelen," *Rotterdams Dagblad*, March 23, 1992.

The only way his successors can build files of their own is by blackmailing homosexuals, and naturally this still goes on.[147]

Eugen, a Bucharest gay man in his twenties, tells the following story:

I was walking in the Opera Park, one night in September 1996, about 1:00 AM. Two policemen stopped to ask me what I was doing there. They asked for my papers; I gave them, but I said, "What do you want? Is it illegal to walk in the park at night?" So they said, "If you think you're so tough, come to the station and we'll talk there."

They took me off to the main police station on Calea Victoriei—the varianta section. They put me in a cell for an hour. Then they photographed me and took my fingerprints, and sat me down with thirty or forty police photographs—front and side shots—and demanded that I say who I recognized. I refused to say. They told me I had better get out of Romania, that I would have a lot of trouble if I stayed. They said: "We will know you. We have a lot of people in photographs here."[148]

In Brasov in October 1996, Sandu V. was summoned from his home by police by officers from the morals section of the municipal police. He was photographed (face and side) and his fingerprints were taken. Police told him he was known to be homosexual—"so don't bother lying"—and asked him about private apartments where homosexuals met in Brasov, as well as men who owned gay pornography.[149] Similarly, in 1996, two men from the town of Valenii de Munte complained to ACCEPT that they had been summoned by a municipal policeman who asked them to inform regularly on other gay men.[150]

Police routinely patrol public places where gay men are known to meet, harassing them regardless of whether the men are actually performing sexual acts or simply trying to associate with others of the same sexual orientation; gay men caught there are sometimes blackmailed. Daniel I. reports:

---

[147] Interview by Scott Long and Bogdan Voicu with Bogdan Dumitrescu, June 1997.

[148] Interview by Scott Long and Yves Nya Ngatchou with Eugen M., June 1997.

[149] Interview by Yves Nya Ngatchou with Sandu V., July 1997.

[150] Interview by Scott Long with Adrian Coman of ACCEPT, June 1997.

> In May 1996, I went with a friend to the toilets in the North Railway Station. One person was prowling around. He opened a cubicle where a man was urinating, and the man told him to get out. The prowler left the toilets; then he came back in a few minutes with his shirt torn, and two policemen following him. He said he had been sexually assaulted.
>
> He must have been working for the police. He would not say who had assaulted him; probably he was waiting till the police found out who had the most resources; then he would point at that person and the negotiations would begin. Everyone who was in the toilet was taken to the police post in the station. They searched us and interrogated us about what we were doing there. My friend and I had the nerve to confront them. We insisted on being interrogated in the presence of the accuser and we demanded that he say which one of us had assaulted him. "Who tore your shirt?" He couldn't answer. And we insisted we were not homosexual and were only there to use the toilet. Finally they let us go. But they warned us that we would be arrested if were seen again in the station. And all the money in our pockets was taken.[151]

Rares A. reports a similar incident in 1995 in the Bucharest railway station toilets. He approached and initiated casual conversation with a man who quickly left the toilets. Moments later, two police came in. He was taken to the station, and information from his ID were recorded. Police interrogated and mocked him for an hour, demanding names of other people who cruised the station. "Because I was a student, they supposed they couldn't get much money from me": however, they took what he had on him.[152]

Two men, asking to remain anonymous, approached the Romanian Helsinki Committee in April 1997 claiming that at another cruising area in Bucharest, a policeman lies in wait and routinely blackmails gay men, threatening to take them to the station to be photographed if they do not pay.[153]

---

[151] Interview by Scott Long with Daniel I. June 1997.

[152] Interview by Scott Long with Rares A., June 1997.

[153] Interview by Scott Long with Ion Iacos of the Romanian Helsinki Committee, June 1997.

In Bucharest, police maintain a visible presence nightly near the Opera Park, the city's main public space in which gay men meet.[154] Beginning in early 1994, organized gangs of at least a dozen people—masked but apparently young—raided the park at night. Wielding either chains or clubs, they swept the park from end to end, beating gay men there. Numerous gay men have reported that the goal seemed to be to drive them toward the police, who waited at the other end of the park, and who refused to respond if victims, threatened or injured, approached them to complain—but would check victims' IDs, recording names and addresses. Police and gangs often appeared to be working in cooperation. Florin Radu described an incident in late 1994:

> Eight of them surrounded me and hit me with chains on the head and face. My head was bleeding so badly that I was dizzy and I could barely see for the blood. When I left the park there were police there. They stopped me and checked my papers. Then they pushed me away and said, "See what happens to *poponarii* like you?"[155]

The attacks reached a peak in 1995, when the gangs appeared in the park two or three nights each week. In 1996 and 1997 they continued, but more sporadically.[156] Similar stories have been recorded elsewhere. A gay man in Timisoara reports that, beginning in mid to late 1996, gangs of twelve to fifteen people—usually without masks, either teenagers or in their early twenties—would sweep the central park there, driving men toward ranks of civil guards who inspected IDs.[157]

Bogdan Dumitrescu describes how Bucharest police monitor one gay meeting place:

---

[154] In the spring of 1997, a private security service, ARGUS—billing itself as a "rapid reaction force" or "antiterrorism unit"—also began stationing a car with tinted windows near the cruising area of the Opera Park at night, possibly to photograph or otherwise identify gay men. Representatives of Human Rights Watch and IGLHRC observed this car repeatedly in June 1997.

[155] Interview by Scott Long with Florin Radu, 1995. The term roughly means "buttfuckers."

[156] Bogdan Voicu to Scott Long, June 1997.

[157] Interview by Scott Long with Silviu in Timisoara, June 1997.

> The Opera Park is split half-and-half between the precincts in Section 3 and Section 17. They patrol the area and if you do not bribe them or come to an understanding you end up at the station writing a statement. The sub-officers are the stupidest and most frightening: they have an eighth-grade education and a bad mentality, and they will beat or abuse you for money.

Law 61/1991 is sometimes used to harass gays in meeting places and elsewhere. On August 15, 1996, at 12:15 AM, Dumitrescu was walking through the Opera Park in a comically exaggerated, effeminate manner which he calls "strutting." Police took him in, demanding whether he thought he was a girl. Dumitrescu (who had long before lost his measure of protection from police interference when Major Catalineanu was promoted) says that at the station, looking for witnesses to his offense, a policeman picked a confiscated ID from a pile: "that was the witness." He was released but in three days received a citation to pay a 25,000 lei fine (approximately $8 in 1996) under Law 61/1991, for "committing obscene acts and gestures."[158]

On January 7, 1997, Dumitrescu says,

> about ten of us were at a birthday party. Over half were gay, with a few straight friends. Between 1:00 and 2:00 a.m. policemen came—regular cops and one from the Health Police; they said they were there because of "public scandal." None of the neighbors had complained, but the police watch this flat because they know a gay man owns it.
>
> We were handcuffed and put in police cars. They searched all our papers—they took my agenda and all my phone numbers. We were taken to Section 3, where the police made jokes about me and read out the names from my agenda. Afterward they said they were putting us in the lockup. I knew this station didn't have a lockup cell; but the investigating officer said, "We have one in the basement now, just for faggots." We were kept there till after noon the next day. They made fun of us constantly. I had to pay a fine of 100,000 lei

---

[158] Proces-verbal B-1693741, politia Sector 5, Bucuresti.

[approximately $40] under Law 61. Another man at the party, who argued with the police, was fined 400,000.[159]

Dan Hutanasu, thirty, of Bucharest, has described an incident to Human Rights Watch and IGLHRC:

> On April 18, 1997, in a bus, I spoke to a man and tried to pick him up. I proposed to give him a blow job. He smiled and said that instead of doing it on the run, we would be better off going to his place. During the conversation, he was very curious to find out more details about me . . .
>
> We locked the door, I sat on the bed. Then he told me he was a cop with the municipal police and that he was going to arrest me. He asked me several times who I was. I pleaded with him to let me go. Two minutes later he took his spray out and sprayed it at me.
>
> I broke the window to run away but there was a metal grid preventing me, so I went for the door. He pushed me against the closet. . . . All along, I didn't hit him. He said he was going to kill me. He started strangling me, he started shouting as though I was attacking him, so the neighbors would come. I succeeded in running away. I ran to the next corner where he caught me. While running after me he was shouting as though I was the attacker. He grabbed my jacket and hit me.
>
> I managed to get away again, leaving my glasses, jacket and my hat in the street. I was dizzy but I stopped a taxi. But the man in the taxi grabbed me and handed me over to the policeman. He took me to the police station—the Bucur Obor station which is a sub-division of Section 8. On the way, he hit me very badly, even worse than I had been hit so far: he broke my lip and I was bleeding from the mouth and the nose.
>
> At the police station . . . I showed my student ID. They all looked at the arresting officer as though this was a delicate matter. It was after midnight. . . . They called the Section 8 headquarters and talked to a

[159] Dosar no. 3970/97, judecatoria Sector 1, Bucuresti.

> captain and asked him what to do with me. I assume the captain suggested a fine. . . . Then they put me in the same room with the police officer. His name was Viorel Jugunaru. He hit me with his fist on the face. I didn't react . . . They had me sign a statement which they dictated to me. I signed since it was true, although it did not mention that I had been beaten, that the man had agreed to having oral sex, that it had happened at his place. All it said was that I propositioned him. The *proces-verbal* carried the maximum possible fine under the law on "soliciting someone to have sexual relations for material profit" [Law 61/1991, Art. 2 (6): the maximum fine is 1 million lei, about $125, more than an average monthly salary]. So now I was a prostitute. That part was not read to me although the law was mentioned, and I didn't ask either. . . . They took me to the Section 8 headquarters and fingerprinted me and photographed me, front and side. They asked me if I was on drugs, if I got money from my "customers." . . . Then they let me go.[160]

Surveillance in Baia-Mare

In 1996 two gay men from Baia-Mare, in northern Romania, contacted the Romanian Helsinki Committee, saying they were fleeing police in their home city who were interrogating numerous men on charges of homosexuality.

IGLHRC investigated this case in September 1996, and Human Rights Watch together with IGLHRC returned to Baia-Mare in June 1997.[161] An atmosphere of intense fear prevails among gay men there; anxieties about surveillance abound. What emerged was a story of a mysterious inquiry, conducted by Liviu Ivan, a colonel in the county police who is reliably reported to work for the successor agency to the Securitate—the greatly feared Communist-era secret police. The inquiry seems driven by political motives and directed at a person or persons in a high position. Numerous gay men were terrorized; one claims to have been severely beaten; another was driven to two suicide attempts.

---

[160] Interview by Yves Nya Ngatchou with Dan Hutasanu, July 1997.

[161] In September 1996 Scott Long and Bogdan Voicu spoke to Daniel D., Georghe I,, Kalman K., Nelu P., Ioan Toporan, Colonel Liviu Ivan and Colonel Botea of the county police, and Chief Prosecutor of the county Eugen Rosca; in June 1997 Long and Voicu spoke to Daniel D., Gheorghe I., Kalman K., Ioan Toporan, prosecutor Ioan Brisc, and various personnel at Policlinica 1 in Baia-Mare, as well as with other persons who wish to remain completely anonymous.

Daniel D., one of the people interrogated, reports that the case began in early 1996 when Colonel Ivan discovered "something to blackmail" two gay men in Baia-Mare, Manix B. and Avram L. Based on what Avram L. told him, he believes the two men were forced to give Ivan names of important people who had engaged in homosexual relations, possibly including persons in the police and/or prosecutor's offices in the city and county.

Ivan, although an officer in the county police, is widely known to have worked for the Securitate—and is widely believed to continue to do so. Employees at Policlinica , Baia-Mare's principal hospital, remember him as having been the Securitate officer responsible for enforcing abortion laws before 1989.[162] Apparently in 1996 Ivan obtained further names of homosexuals by searching the hospital files for patients treated for sexually transmitted diseases, or STDs (it is reported that he attempted to intimidate hospital officials) and finding the case of a policeman, Flaminius L., who contracted syphilis and infected two other gay men.[163]

In a manner reminiscent of police procedures in Sibiu three years before, Ivan then began calling in others. Gheorghe I., twenty-three, remembers that in March 1996, he stepped outside the shop where he worked and was approached by Manix B., an acquaintance, as if to point him out. Suddenly "a voice behind me said, 'I am Colonel Ivan.'" He was questioned for five hours, with Ivan telling him, "If you want to go home, you have to tell us with whom, where, and when you had sex, where you hide your pornography, and where you got it." His address book was taken, and he was interrogated about the names in it. Ivan also took him to his home and conducted a search, taking all his letters and a passport.[164] Further threats at the station followed, and he was made to write a statement with the few names of sexual contacts he reluctantly gave.

At home, that night, Gheorghe took an overdose of sleeping pills. His mother rushed him to the hospital, where for two days he suffered from partial amnesia

---

[162] Conversation by Scott Long and Bogdan Voicu with Nurse Carmen Barbolovici, and interview with Dr. asist. Grigor, Dermatology Department of Policlinica 1, June 1997. Other informants have reported that Colonel Ivan had a reputation for engaging in abusive behavior, including blackmail, towards women who sought abortion.

[163] See "rezolutie" in dosar no. 61/P/1996, Parchetul de pe langa Tribunalul Maramures; confirmed by Dr. Grigor. Copies of this and other documents are on file with Human Rights Watch and IGLHRC.

[164] No warrant from a prosecutor was shown—a procedure required by Articles 104 and 216-219 of the c criminal procedural code.

about the interrogation. Within hours of his return home, a flood of memories returned. He went to the bath and slashed his wrists. His mother found him swimming in blood. Again she saved his life.

Ivan came to the workplace of Daniel D., twenty-five, while he was away; Ivan searched his possessions and told Daniel's colleagues he was under investigation for homosexuality. When his colleagues told him of the visit, Daniel went voluntarily to the county police. Ivan's first question to him was, "Do you like anal sex?" He demanded the names of at least forty sexual contacts before he would let Daniel leave. After four hours of intense interrogation, Ivan searched his apartment, without a warrant; Daniel had destroyed all compromising materials before leaving.

Nelu P., forty, is a married businessman whose wife does not know of his bisexuality. In April 1996, Colonel Ivan came to Nelu's shop. Uniquely, in this case, he took the precaution of bringing a warrant signed by a prosecutor, perhaps expecting Nelu to be conversant with legal procedure. The mandate, however, only authorized the search of Nelu's home—not the office, which Ivan proceeded to rifle.[165] He confiscated a magazine hidden there, "designed for those who practice sexual relations between persons of the same sex,"[166] along with an address book and numerous letters. Nelu was then taken in for an eight-hour interrogation, during which Ivan kicked and beat him, demanding to know "how he did it and with whom." Manix B. was also produced, to allege before Nelu that the two had had sexual relations. Nelu was released, but underwent two more interrogations in the next two weeks in what he calls "psychological warfare." Ivan threatened to tell Nelu's wife; he commanded Nelu to call the numbers in his address book, and, when he refused, struck him "many times" on the top of his head with his fist. He suffered continuous verbal abuse and says that when he left the station after the last interrogation, he had been beaten so badly in the back and spine that he could hardly walk.

Kalman K., thirty-one, lived in a village in the county. Ivan picked him up there and took him to the police at Baia-Mare. Kalman was shown a list of forty to fifty names, including prominent people in the county, and told to identify sexual contacts. At first, he named only two: Flaminius L. and a man who had later emigrated. Ivan then demanded extensive details of these sexual experiences, and pressed for others, particularly insisting that he name his friend Gheorghe I. as his lover (a detail both deny). When he refused, two officers pushed him against the wall and physically menaced him until he agreed.

---

[165] Authorizatie de perchezitie 61/P/1996, 3 April 1996.

[166] Proces-verbal of the search, found in dosar 61/P/1996 by Human Rights Watch and IGLHRC in June 1997.

When released, Kalman immediately contacted Gheorghe. He believes that Ivan was preparing to arrest both of them. They fled to Bucharest and told their story to the Romanian Helsinki Committee.

A newspaper reporter, Ioan Toporan, was a friend of some of those interrogated. In late April, to call attention to their situation, he published a short account of the investigation:

> The life of the "boys apart" has been broken up by a colonel with the name of a Tsar. Picked up from office or home, after a painstaking search (without a warrant), the victims . . . were taken to the police station, where they were kept five to seven hours, in order to obtain "confessions" and of course lists of other victims to come . . . Is [the investigation] aimed at nameless persons highly placed in the county?[167]

He was immediately summoned to the county police. There, the press officer demanded his sources, saying, "If you do not tell us, we cannot ensure your protection—a car can hit you, someone can stick a knife in you in a dark street."[168] Toporan refused.

Two articles in succession appeared in another local newspaper, under the headline "Guessing game: Who are the twelve homosexuals who have scandalized Baia?" They promised to reveal the names of those implicated: "Who are these kissing homos? . . . When we publish a list of these 12, there will be a lot of shame. . . On the subject of these 12 homosexuals there exists a criminal file." And in a thinly veiled, vulgar threat: " What does a cock have to do with the Prefect's office?"[169] The pseudonymous articles were, Toporan says, "a warning to somebody." Full revelation was promised in a third article, which never came—because, Toporan believes, "Someone in power intervened to prevent it."

Many of those interrogated remained under surveillance. Gheorghe I. states that a man came up to him in July 1996 and whispered that he had been following

---

[167] Ioan Toporan, "200 e un articol," *Nord magazin*, April 12-21, 1996.

[168] Toporan also claims that, months later, Ivan threatened to frame him with a concocted statement accusing him of rape.

[169] "?Ghicitoare: cine-s cei 12 homosexuali care au scandalizat Baia?" and "Cine-s cel 12 pupaciosi homo care au scandalizat Baia?" *Graiul Maramuresului* , May 5 and May 19, 1996; the articles were signed "E. Pidosnicu" (a complicated pun in Romanian). The Prefect is the highest authority of the county.

Gheorghe for two weeks. Nelu P. says that he received anonymous letters and phone calls threatening to reveal his homosexuality; that he believes his telephone to have been tapped; and that he was often followed in Baia-Mare by a black car which he could recognize by its license plates.

Even the total number of those interrogated is uncertain. Kalman K. says there were dozens of names on the list of homosexuals Colonel Ivan showed him. The newspaper articles cited the number 12; and Nelu P., who asked an attorney acquaintance to make inquiries, says he also heard that 12 were directly implicated.

The Romanian Helsinki Committee protested to the Ministry of the Interior, on behalf of Kalman K. and Gheorghe I. The General Inspectorate of Police responded in two letters: one said that the investigation resulted from the discovery of "a group of persons who had entered into homosexual relations"; the other, that the investigation was undertaken after complaints that Manix B. forced a minor to engage in homosexual sex; the minor "also named other homosexuals."[170]

The latter story was repeated to IGLHRC during a meeting in September 1996 with Colonel Ivan and his superior, Colonel Botea of the county police. "All those interrogated," they said, "were in the same group of homosexuals." They confirmed that the alleged aggressor was still at liberty.

It is unlikely that this alleged crime motivated the investigation—not least because, of those persons interrogated who spoke to IGLHRC, all affirmed that Colonel Ivan had not once asked about it, nor had rape or sexual relations with minors been brought up at all. Colonel Ivan's sole concern had been to extort more names of homosexuals. Indeed, Manix B., far from being a suspect, was called in at Nelu P.'s interrogation as a privileged witness, and was also used to identify Gheorghe I. The very fact that he remained at liberty is itself revealing, in a system where pre-trial detention is routinely used to jail most suspects. If evidence of the alleged crime existed at all, it would appear that it was used simply to turn Manix B. into an informer; and that investigation of a possible serious offence was abandoned in favor of a witchhunt against innocent persons. If a criminal act did take place, it did so with impunity, in order that Colonel Ivan might carry on a task perceived as more important—identifying and harassing other homosexuals.

On September 26, 1996, IGLHRC met with Eugen Rosca, chief prosecutor of the county. Rosca staged a theatrical display of surprise, asserting he had never heard of the case; calling for the file—which contained only one slip of paper, the mandate issued by the prosecutor to search Nelu P.'s house; claiming that he had known nothing about this search; and insisting that he would himself launch an

---

[170] IGP, Grupul de Control, letter no. 44.719, July 22, 1996; Comitetul pentru Drepturile Omului, letter no. 12.577, May 13, 1995.

investigation into how Colonel Ivan and the county police had conducted a criminal probe, in violation of Romanian criminal procedure, without the knowledge of the county prosecutor.

These statements were almost certainly untrue. Returning in June 1997, IGLHRC representatives succeeded in seeing the file again. It was still virtually empty; but it now contained a document, dated September *27,* 1996—the day after the departure of the prior IGLHRC team—called a "Resolution": a hasty attempt by prosecutors to cover their tracks and devise with a story to explain the investigation. The document stated that the investigation had been initiated by an inquiry into transmission of syphilis by Flaminius L.[171] Human Rights Watch and IGLHRC received confirmation from hospital officials that this syphilis case dated from 1993—hardly a justification for interrogations which began only in 1996. Nor were any of those victims who spoke to IGLHRC asked about transmission of disease through sexual contact..[172] It also mentioned the allegations against Manix B., but confusingly offered no connection between that case and the syphilis transmission. "From the contents of the investigation," the document states, "it emerged that, within the city of Baia-Mare, there exists an organized network of men who have practiced unnatural sexual relations. The number of these persons is approximately twenty to thirty."

Finally, exploiting the status of Flaminius L.—who worked at the penitentiary and hence fell under military discipline—it refers the entire matter to the regional Military Prosecutor, based in the city of Oradea.[173]

---

[171] Knowing transmission of sexually transmitted diseases (STDs) is criminalized by Article 309 of the penal code (see next chapter); probably this detail was partly an attempt to shift the public record of the investigation away from the controversial Article 200.

[172] Human Rights Watch and IGLHRC were allowed to examine hospital records by staff in the Dermatology Section, Policlinica 1.

[173] The exact contents and whereabouts of the full file in the case (which holds, as a note in the 1997 file specifies, seventy-nine documents, including letters seized from Nelu and Gheorghe) are also mysterious. On September 26, 1996, Colonel Ivan told IGLHRC that the file had *already* been sent to the military prosecutor in Oradea. Yet the documents shown IGLHRC in June 1997 contain a note from chief prosecutor Rosca formally sending the file to Oradea—a note also dated the day *after* the departure of IGLHRC's mission in 1996. And several days after that departure, Daniel D. was shown a large file (containing his previous statements given to Ivan) while being interrogated again by a county prosecutor—indicating the file was still in Baia-Mare. It seems likely that police and prosecutors, anxious to conceal the evidence, will consistently claim the file is in some place other than where human-rights investigators happen to be.

A few days after IGLHRC representatives left Baia-Mare in September 1996, Daniel D. was summoned by Rosca's subordinate, prosecutor Ioan Brisc—in apparent retaliation for Daniel's conversations with IGLHRC. Brisc asked who he had been "gossiping with" lately, demanding whether he picked up "clients" in the restaurant where he worked, and sneering, "Why are you allowed to handle food? You are a danger to society." He ordered Daniel to reaffirm the statement he had given Colonel Ivan. Daniel refused, saying the statement had been given under duress. Though Brisc threatened to charge him under Article 200, he finally was allowed to leave.

The language of the articles placed in the Baia-Mare press, with their allusions to the Prefect's office, suggests that a highly placed official or officials may have been the ultimate target of Colonel Ivan's interrogations. Several of those questioned were asked whether they knew homosexuals in state employment; and Ioan Toporan maintains that he has been confidentially told that an attempt to blackmail or destroy the career of a person in authority motivated the investigation. What is certain is that Colonel Ivan, trained in Ceausescu's secret police to punish illegal abortions, found in Article 200 a legal pretext to apply the same invasive and abusive procedures against gay men.

Police Beatings and Torture

Physical abuse of prisoners by police remains common throughout Romania. Documentation collected by IGLHRC and Human Rights Watch, however, suggests a longstanding pattern of meting out special abuse to those suspected of homosexuality. In addition to mistreatment directly at the hands of police and guards, cases such as those of Ciprian Cucu and Marian Mutascu, and of Ovidiu Chetea, Nicolae Petricas, and Nicolae Stupariu, above, show that beatings and rapes by other inmates are performed, with the collusion or even encouragement of the authorities.

Many cases previously discussed show abuses directed by police against those arrested under Article 200, paragraph 1. Other examples show how those arrested, rightly or wrongly, under other paragraphs of Article 200 also suffer from the presumption of homosexuality—and how violence may be used to extract confessions.

Ienel Sandu was nineteen when he was arrested in 1990 in a village near Tecuci; he later spoke hesitantly and painfully about the events to IGLHRC representatives. By his own account, after wedding festivities he attended, another man (previously imprisoned for homosexuality under Ceausescu) followed him and invited him to have sexual relations. Sandu suggested coming indoors; the man refused, insisting they perform the act outside. Unable to resolve their differences, they parted, and Sandu went home alone.

The next morning, Sandu was arrested: the other man had reported that Sandu had beaten him and forced him to perform oral sex. Sandu states that village police cursed him as a homosexual, and beat him from 7:00 AM to 8:00 PM, with truncheons on the torso and the back, as well as on the hands and feet. After thirteen hours, he "confessed." He was dragged, barely conscious, to a doctor, who sent him out, and—according to Sandu—"examined" the police in private for fifteen minutes, then signed a clean certificate of his health. He was sentenced to four years under Article 200, paragraph 2.[174]

Nita Manea was arrested in 1991, when he was twenty. Convicted, with two others, of having forced sexual relations with an eighteen-year-old in Slobozia, he denies the charge. He reports that after his arrest he was beaten for several hours, on the stomach and on the palms of his hands, to extract a confession; police shouted "homosexual" and insulting phrases at him during the beatings, and threatened to rape him "as a homosexual rapes children."[175]

Marcel Brosca was nineteen and a student when arrested in March 1992. He overslept on a train trip, waking in a town called Tecuci. There was no other train that night, so he slept in the station waiting room. He was wakened by policemen, accompanied by a seventeen-year-old boy, who—after some hesitation—pointed at Brosca and told the police, "Him."

Brosca was beaten in the station police post for three or four hours. His hair was pulled; the sides and back of his head were struck against table and wall till blood poured over his face; his arms were bent and stretched; and the soles of his feet were bastinadoed. He fainted at least three times. He was not given any idea of the charges for the first two hours; eventually he was read the accuser's declaration, stating he had been forced by a stranger to perform oral sex on the train. More beatings followed, during which Brosca was explicitly mocked for homosexuality, until he signed a statement dictated by police. At his trial, he repudiated this statement. However, he was convicted under Article 200, paragraphs 1 and 2.[176]

---

174 Sandu, who when visited by IGLHRC representatives in Galati penitentiary was extremely frail and weak, with severely impaired vision, seemed an unlikely candidate to overpower anyone. Interview by Razvan Ion and Scott Long with Ienel Sandu, Galati penitentiary, January 1993.

175 Interview by Razvan Ion and Scott Long with Nita Manea, Galati penitentiary, January 1993.

176 Interview by Razvan Ion and Scott Long with Marcel Brosca, Galati penitentiary, January 1993.

Doru Marian Beldie was arrested in July 1992, not long after turning nineteen. He reports that, for over a week not long previously, he had had a sexual relationship for a week with another boy, whom he says was sixteen or seventeen. The parents of the other boy discovered the relationship, and reported Beldie to the police. He was taken to the Section 17 police station in Bucharest, where he was beaten severely—with truncheons on the flats of the hands and feet—for three or four hours, until he signed a confession. The policeman most active in beating him, named Lebedov, repeatedly called him a "stinking homosexual pervert" and other names.[177]

Elizov Nemaceac was twenty-eight when arrested in 1994. He was ultimately convicted under Article 200, paragraph 2 for forcing another man to have sexual relations.

Nemaceac—who denies being homosexual—admits the essence of the charges. He also states, however, that when he was arrested and taken to the municipal police station in Constanta, he was not given food or water for three days. Police told him he was being treated as a homosexual deserved to be treated. He survived by drinking water from the toilets. He was beaten by Lt. Marius Tocman, who called him a "European pervert."[178]

Dumitru Abalaesi was arrested in 1995 in Chisinau Cris, for forcing a fellow shepherd to have sexual relations. Police hung him in a position colloquially called the "*macavela*": stringing him up facing the wall, they beat him with a broomstick for two hours till he signed the statement they wanted. They threatened to rape Abalaesi with the broomstick, telling him "a homosexual should like to take it." Next day, taken to see the prosecutor, he refused to sign a typed version of the same statement. He showed the prosecutor the bruises on his back; his own court-appointed lawyer joked about what the backs of homosexuals should look like. The four policemen who had beaten him the day before started hitting him, in the head, stomach, and ribs, before the prosecutor; then they took him to the cellar of the courthouse and beat him till he agreed to sign.[179]

---

[177] Interview by Razvan Ion and Scott Long with Doru Marian Beldie, Jilava penitentiary, January 1993; interview by Scott Long, Yves Nya Ngatchou, and Bogdan Voicu with Beldie, Gherla penitentiary, December 1993.

[178] Interview by Vera Campeanu and Scott Long with Elizov Nemaceac, Poarta Alba penitentiary, June 1997; dosar no. 2992/1995, judecatoria Constanta.

[179] Interview by Scott Long, Mona Nicoara, and Bogdan Voicu with Dumitru Abalaesi, Arad penitentiary, June 1997. Abalaesi says one of the policemen was named Harmigiu.

Homosexuality in Detention

Although self-identified homosexuals in prison are subjected to isolation, rape, and other forms of maltreatment by their fellow inmates—as attested by both former prisoners and by prison officials[180]— homosexual activity remains widespread throughout the penitentiary system. One veteran of Romanian penitentiaries, who has been imprisoned over a dozen times, says that homosexual relations are "the only form of joy" in the prisons.[181]

All sexual activity between prisoners is punishable by administrative sanction in the Romanian system. However, whereas a heterosexual couple in a mixed prison might receive a notation in their penitentiary files, and possible sanctions such as isolation, Article 200 makes homosexual relations liable to additional, invidious criminal punishment, generally resulting in more time being added to the participants' sentences. Convictions for so widespread an activity are necessarily occasional; yet selective prosecutions do take place. They appear to single out and make examples of prisoners unpopular with administrators, to receive additional sentences and serve additional time.

Marius Aitai, who in 1992, with two other prisoners, received an additional sentence of two and one half years for having consensual sex in Gherla penitentiary,[182] told IGLHRC representatives:

> I was punished three times for this. I had a sanction placed in my file; I was put in isolation for ten days—where they fed me every other day and the guards beat me constantly; and then, six months after it happened, they told me they were going to put me in a criminal trial.

---

[180] Interviews with Colonel Zinca in Galati; testimony of Ciprian Cucu; interviews with Ovidiu Banu, Florin Hopris, and Ciprian Stoica; interview by Scott Long, Mona Nicoara, and Bogdan Voicu with Col. Marian Bucur, director of Arad penitentiary, June 1997.

[181] Interview by Scott Long and Yves Nya Ngatchou with Gheorghe Ioan, January 1995.

[182] Sentinta penala 733/1992, judecatoria Dej. One of the prisoners actually received three years. Owing to procedures for combining sentences Aitai in fact had six months added to his term.

> Prisoners have no rights when they go to trial. I never saw a lawyer before or during the trial.[183]

In another case, in April 1995, Ionel Penciu, seventeen, was in Tulcea penitentiary, sharing a transit cell with five other prisoners, mostly minors. He entered into an affair with one prisoner, Tudorel Retea, seventeen, over a three-week period. Another inmate, Nicolae Raducanu, who was eighteen, also had sexual relations with Retea.

According to Penciu, two older prisoners discovered these relations, and blackmailed him to give them clothes and other goods, threatening to report the three. Finally they did inform the guards.

At first, as exculpation, Retea claimed he had been forced to have sex; later, court records show, he retracted this.[184] Penciu claims to have been beaten "very severely" by guards. All three were put on trial. Penciu and Retea were tried under Article 200, paragraph 1, and had one year and six months added to their sentences; Raducanu was tried under paragraph 2—because as an adult he had sex with Retea, a seventeen-year-old minor—and received three years.[185] Although the case took place well after the Constitutional Court's 1994 decision, the court file makes absolutely no effort to establish that the acts "caused public scandal": the file makes no mention of the conditions for prosecution imposed by the court.

Some prisoners allege that authorities concoct charges of homosexuality as punishment. Viorel-Daniel Munteanu was seventeen when arrested in Petrosani in January 1993, for burglary. What he ultimately received, however, was a three-year sentence under Article 200, paragraph 2, for forcing a fellow inmate to have sex with him in the police lockup in Petrosani. [186]

---

[183] Interview by Scott Long, Yves Nya Ngatchou, and Bogdan Voicu with Marius Aitai, Gherla penitentiary, December 1993; interview by Long and Nya Ngatchou with Aitai, Gherla, January 1995.

[184] A short summary of the trial in the file—dosar nr. 3766/1995, judecatoria Tulcea—shows that Retea stated "that these relations happen all the time in Tulcea penitentiary, that no one was forced, and that it should not be a matter for condemnation."

[185] Sentinta penala 1219/1996, judecatoria Tulcea; interview by Scott Long and Bogdan Voicu with Ionel Penciu, Aiud penitentiary, July 1997.

[186] Sentinta penala no.2114/1994, judecatoria Deva.

Munteanu admits the theft of videocassettes which led to his first arrest; in fact, he turned himself in at the police station in Petrosani. A delegation of police from Brad were visiting Petrosani, looking for a group of thieves they believed had fled there. They took an interest in Munteanu's case, and offered to help interrogate him. They did this by abusing him severely. As soon as the local investigator left the room, the Brad police twisted his fingers and tore at the flesh of his thighs with pliers; they beat him with a heavy wire spring; they hit him in the face with a large fiberglass bar, forcing it in his mouth to try to knock his teeth out; and they beat him over the back with a shovel. The beatings continued for four hours.

For ten days afterward, Munteanu was periodically beaten in the police lockup by local police, but never as seriously as the first day. Two months later, his father filed a complaint.

He maintains that the charge of homosexual rape was concocted out of a fight he and another detainee had with a cellmate. The cellmate then testified that Munteanu and the other detainee raped him; the other detainee was not charged because he agreed to testify against Munteanu. Munteanu believes police persuaded the cellmate to accuse him, to punish him for complaining about the initial beatings.[187]

[187] Interview by Scott Long, Mona Nicoara, and Yves Nya Ngatchou with Viorel Daniel Munteanu, Deva penitentiary, January 1995.

8. LAW, MEDICINE, AND SEXUALITY

Before 1989 few Romanian psychologists had access to current medical information on human sexuality, or knew—for example— that the World Psychiatric Association had removed homosexuality from its roster of mental illnesses in 1971.[188] Homosexuals were sometimes given "behavioral treatments," including electroshock aversion therapy combined with tranquilizers "to make the subject cooperative."[189]

All the same, psychiatrists interviewed by Human Rights Watch and IGLHRC agreed that homosexuality has historically not been treated primarily as a medical issue in Romania. Dr. Valerian Tuculescu, founder of the Association of Free Psychiatrists—an organization to assist survivors of psychiatric abuse—says that "during the dictatorship, the official line was that in a healthy socialist society like ours, homosexuality—like suicide, say, or alcoholism—did not exist."[190]

Psychiatric and psychological discourse on homosexuality remains confused, operating in a welter of contradictory definitions and forced distinctions—as one forensic report put it, "between homosexuality as panaphilia (perversion—sexual deviation), a property of the psychopath, and homosexuality as a neurotic phenomenon; that is to say, between homosexuality developing or being developed in the frame of a psychiatric affliction, and passing homosexuality, due to circumstances."[191] Even psychiatrists who deny that homosexuality is a personality disorder may do so in order to condemn it rather than to urge toleration. One psychiatrist who campaigned against modifying Article 200 did so on the grounds that "homosexuality is not a mental illness, it does not have a genetic, hormonal, or psychiatric cause, and therefore no medical cause. It can be considered a vice, and

---

[188] Interview by Long and Voicu with Dr. Valerian Tuculescu, June 1997. The WPA's Diagnostic and Statistical Manual (III) was finally translated into Romanian in 1993.

[189] Interview by Vera Campeanu and Scott Long with Dr. Aurel Romila, June 1997. Romila insists, though, that such treatments were carried out infrequently, and only on voluntary subjects.

[190] Interview by Long and Voicu with Dr. Tuculescu, June 1997.

[191] Forensic-psychiatric report on Traian Pasca by the County Forensic Laboratory, Alba, 712/IV/46/15.04.1993.

like any other vice it has a sure and deleterious influence on the individual himself, as well as on his family and the integrity of society."[192]

However, emerging medical perspectives—and stereotypes—have affected the legal treatment of homosexuality. The distinction mentioned above, between permanent and transient homosexuality, was often referred to by officials Human Rights Watch and IGLHRC interviewed—generally to justify penalizing one kind, or both. One prosecutor referred to "cases of homosexuality where people experience a genuine need, an intimate problem: for instance, the delicate situation of those who commit homosexual acts in penitentiaries. These were isolated people, who were driven to homosexuality temporarily, from necessity. There are circumstances to extenuate their deeds, unlike perverts in freedom, who perform this thing for enjoyment, as a hobby."[193]

Persons arrested under Article 200 are still automatically subject to psychiatric examination; these examinations account for homosexuality by "lack of behavioral inhibitions and psychomotor excitement influenced by alcohol consumption, with the effect of suppressing moral censures"; or "sexual inhibitions owing to fixation on a perverse stage, or owing to a complex homosexualism."[194] One suspect showed: "Defensive attitude . . . Instinctive level: sexual impulses exacerbated by predominant attraction to persons of the same sex, taking the aspect of manifest homosexuality, apparently passive and of an egodystonic model. Anxiety."[195] The purpose of these examinations is unclear; it is certainly not to recommend leniency on medical grounds.

---

[192] Dr. Rodica Nastase, "Homosexualitate privita din punct de vedere psihiatric," in *Homosexuality: propaganda a degenerarii umane*, pamphlet of the Asociatia Studentilor Crestin-Ortodox din Romania (ASCOR), 1995.

[193] Interview by Long and Voicu with Prosecutor Luha, Alba, July 1997.

[194] Forensic-psychiatric reports on Mariana Cetiner by the County Forensic Laboratory, Alba, 3034/IV/261/18.10.1995; and by the "Prof. Mina Minovici" Forensic Institute, Bucharest, A6/16/760.

[195] Forensic-psychiatric report on Pasca. "Anxiety" and "defensiveness," of course, might also be taken as natural responses to imprisonment, particularly (as in this case) in the immediate wake of being raped.

Physical examinations of the anal and genital regions of men arrested for homosexuality are also common. These examinations are generally spurious, relying on the idea that anal sex leaves lasting "lesions" around the anus or "modifications" on the penis. Often involving retracting the foreskin and the insertion of instruments into the anus, they are profoundly degrading and humiliating to those forced to undergo them.[196] The pain and humiliation which these forced examinations cause place them in violation of numerous international covenants. Article 7 of the International Covenant on Civil and Political Rights, and Article 3 of the European Convention for the Protection of Human Rights and Fundamental Freedoms, prohibit cruel, inhuman, or degrading treatment. Article 16 of the Convention Against Torture and other Cruel, Inhuman or Degrading Treatment or Punishment requires states to prevent such treatment when committed by or performed with the acquiescence of public officials.

A medical issue with profound implications for the legal treatment of homosexuality has been HIV. General Paun of the IGP told Human Rights Watch and IGLHRC: "In 1989, AIDS and other sexually transmitted diseases were very rare in Romania."[197] Such statements betray remarkable amnesia (as well as ignorance about the mechanics and demographics of HIV transmission, which in Romania has not primarily taken place through sexual contact). In fact, failure to monitor the blood supply, shortages of needles and neglect of basic hygiene, and a ubiquitous practice of giving small blood transfusions to children in orphanages and other total institutions, all meant that after the Revolution Romania's pediatric AIDS crisis became an international scandal. Nonetheless, a prevalent rhetoric still depicts AIDS as an external threat, and homosexuals as its internal agents.[198]

---

[196] See particularly the accounts of Vasiliu and Presnac, and of Ciprian Cucu, above. In Cucu's case the examination was not performed until he and Mutascu had been jailed separately for over two weeks—making it blatantly medically useless as an evaluation of their relationship (although each had been raped and sexually abused by other prisoners in the police lockup).

[197] Interview by Campeanu and Long with General Paun, June 1997.

[198] Dr. Maria Georgescu of the Asociatia Romana Anti-SIDA (Romanian Anti-AIDS Association) told Human Rights Watch and IGLHRC, "HIV has completely infected the political discourse about homosexuality by now. Everyone treats an issue of civil rights as if it were one of sanitation." Interview with Vera Campeanu and Scott Long, June 1997.

Justifying a 1993 arrest under Article 200, a police gazette proclaimed, "AIDS is knocking at our portals: launching an SOS is absolutely necessary."[199]

As homosexuality becomes inextricably associated with disease, laws on disease transmission can also be used to monitor and control suspected homosexuals.

On March 30, 1994, Maj. Vasile Ionescu of the police in the town of Fagaras appeared at Attila Horvath's door. He reassured Horvath's terrified mother: "We only suspect your son of having AIDS." Horvath, thirty-five, was told he had had sexual relations "with a number of people" and that he represented a "public danger." Ionescu hinted that he had a direct order from the mayor of Fagaras for Horvath's detention. Horvath was taken to the hospital in Fagaras. Without asking his consent, blood was taken: Ionescu said he would be informed of the results in months. He was never notified.[200]

Over two years later, on July 4, 1996, Ionescu and Plutonier Cornel Folea[201] visited Corneliu Renghea, twenty-two, a student and friend of Attila Horvath. They ordered him to the station the next morning.

The next day, Renghea says, the two officers asked whether he suspected he was HIV-positive. Citing his right to privacy, he declined to answer. The officers refused to let him speak to a lawyer; instead, Renghea says, they began "pulling down law-books, looking for a law they could arrest me under."[202]

Renghea was handcuffed and taken to the Fagaras hospital. This time, however, hospital staff refused to administer an HIV test without Renghea's permission. In an angry confrontation with the officers, Renghea refused. A hospital nurse remembers the officers as "offensive, threatening, and abusive, to him and to us."[203] Renghea was returned to the station, where Ionescu, warning he would be prosecuted, pressured him unsuccessfully to name sexual contacts. Ionescu dictated a statement that Renghea had refused to cooperate with the police. Finally, he was released. However, police offered their version to a local newspaper, which published an article—headlined "An AIDS patient infects young

---

199 Horodinca, "Anuntul miserios," *Tim-polis,* February 1993.

200 Interview by Scott Long and Bogdan Voicu with Attila Horvath, July 1997.

201 *Plutonier* is a junior officer's rank.

202 Interview by Scott Long and Bogdan Voicu with Corneliu Renghea, July 1997.

203 Interview by Scott Long and Bogdan Voicu with Mariana Aros, July 1997.

girls"—describing Renghea in a way which made him readily identifiable, and deploring his "cynicism."[204]

Renghea complained to the League for the Defense of Human Rights (LADO), which wrote to local police officials about the two cases. Fagaras police responded, "Though you are indifferent to the situation of the great majority of youth of good faith who can be contaminated with this virus, we are not . . . How do you defend the human right to health and life? By hiding the truth? Lying to society? Ignoring a state of peril which imperils everyone?" Police also maintained that the inquiry into Horvath's case had been initiated by a letter to the mayor from one Florin Blendea; and that Renghea had been accused by an anonymous letter, a copy of which they released. They also revealed—two years late—that Horvath had tested negative for HIV.[205]

Contacted by Human Rights Watch and IGLHRC, Blendea—an old friend of Horvath—was incredulous at the idea of Horvath's being HIV-positive, and categorically denied having informed on him. As for Renghea's case, Articles 222 and 223 of the criminal procedural code specifically forbid pursuing anonymous complaints. (Asked about this, an extremely nervous Plutonier Folea of the Fagaras police said, "We followed the spirit of the law, not the letter.")[206] The letter claims to be from a young women whose only sexual partner, Renghea, told her he was bisexual; she later tested HIV-positive.[207] Renghea denies that he is bisexual or HIV-positive, and insists no one he knows could have written the letter; he believes police themselves may have forged the letter in the wake of LADO's complaints, to justify their actions.

Neither Renghea nor Horvath is homosexual. However, comments during their interrogations indicate police suspected they were. Horvath was picked up after an acrimonious divorce from the daughter of Fagaras' mayor; he believes the investigation was an attempt to humiliate and discredit him. In turn, Renghea believes that police suspect him of sexual relations with Horvath.

---

[204] Lucia Baki, "Un bolnav de SIDA infesteaza tinerele fete," *Buna ziua Fagaras,* July 22-30, 1996.

[205] Politia Municipiului Fagaras, 135158/13.08.1996; Inspectoratul de Politie al Judetului Brasov, 1775/22.08.1996.

[206] Interviews by Scott Long and Bogdan Voicu with Florin Blendea and Plutonier Cornel Folea, luly 1997.

[207] Letter registered as 143.381 with Fagaras police.

Police justified their attempts to force HIV tests by citing Article 309 of the 1968 penal code, which punished with six months' to three years' imprisonment "transmission of a venereal disease through sexual relations, through sexual relations with persons of the same sex, or through an act of sexual perversion, by a person who knows him/herself to suffer from such a disease." In the new penal code, parliament added a provision specifically penalizing transmission "of AIDS, by a person who knows him/herself to suffer from this disease," with five to fifteen years' imprisonment.[208]

Confidentiality of medical information is also fragile in Romania. Hospital staff, in violation of Ministry of Health regulations, often reveal persons' HIV status to a press eager for scandal; they are seldom if ever punished. [209] In 1996 Cristian Giulan, twenty, of Brasov, attempted suicide in the wake of testing positive for HIV. He woke in the hospital, with a TV crew from the largest national network filming him. Footage of a "homosexual AIDS victim" was broadcast nationally.

---

[208] The old version of Article 309, according to the IGP, rarely led to imprisonment; persons found to carry STDs were usually forcibly impounded in clinics. No one is apparently yet serving a sentence for knowing transmission of HIV; however, according to General Paun, a woman is now under arrest and facing trial for the offense. Captain Cojocaru elaborated that "six or eight persons raped a girl, who was already infected with HIV. They were convicted under Article 197; she is charged with transmitting AIDS to some of them." Human Rights Watch and IGLHRC were unable to discover more about this extremely disturbing case.

[209] Order 1201/16.10.1990 of the Ministry of Health instructs all health institutions "to take necessary measures for strictly respecting the professional secrecy and confidentiality of the diagnosis, which is communicated only to the patient, or in cases of children only to the parents and legal guardians." Order 912/11.9.1992 states that "the activity of informing about HIV infection shall be performed so as to respect anonymity and professional secrecy."

In 1995 the Ministry of Health proposed requiring bi-annual HIV testing, regardless of consent, for persons in certain "risk groups," including medical personnel, dialysis patients, pregnant women, prisoners, prostitutes, and "members of sexual minorities." (Directia Generala a Medicinei Preventive si Promovarea Sanatatii, comunicat no. 11406/13.05.1995). The measure was never implemented, but there is evidence that testing of inmates in the penitentiary goes on in a random fashion, at the point of entry or later, without consent and in some cases without explanation or subsequent notification. (Interviews by Scott Long, Yves Nya Ngatchou, and Bogdan Voicu with Dr. Constantin Ouatu, Iasi penitentiary, and Dr. Paul Duma, Deva penitentiary, June 1997.)

No investigation was ever launched into which hospital personnel had notified the TV station, or admitted the crew to the ward.[210]

Other forms of medical information are also disseminated. In 1995, Iulian M. applied to receive a sex-change operation.[211] Within weeks of his first interview with doctors, an account of his case appeared in a national magazine, with enough details—including his initials—for him to be readily identifiable. He states that only the doctors could have revealed the information. As a consequence, Iulian lost his job.[212]

---

210 Interview by Daniel Iorga, Scott Long, and Bogdan Voicu with Cristian Giulan, July 1997.

211 The first sex-change operation was performed in Romania in 1994, amid frenzied publicity. None has been performed since, though one doctor states that seventeen or eighteen persons are receiving either pre-operative counseling or hormone treatments. (Interview by Scott Long and Bogdan Voicu with Dr. Cristian Bengescu, June 1997.) Amid the general restrictiveness of Romanian laws on sexuality, it is interesting that new legislation—law 119/1996—creates a procedure for postoperative transsexuals to change their legal identity, a provision more liberal than many Western European states possess.

212 Interview by Scott Long and Bogdan Voicu with Iulian M., June 1997.

9. INTERNATIONAL LAW AND DETAILED RECOMMENDATIONS

As this report shows, Article 200 of the Romanian penal code violates international human rights standards. By subjecting to prosecution sexual relations between persons of the same sex that "produce a public scandal" (paragraph 1) and criminalizing incitment or encouragment "to the practice of sexual relations between persons of the same sex, as well as propaganda or association or any other act of proselytism committed in the same scope" (paragraph 5), Article 200 opens the door to severe and arbitrary curtailment of virtually all civil and political rights of gay men and lesbians in the name of popular prejudice. This article not only violates international standards prohibiting discrimination and restricting a government's interference with the right to privacy, it violates the right to expression, association, and assembly, by subjecting to possible prosecution any public manifestation of or supportive speech about homosexuality, as well as organizations or even gatherings of gays and lesbians.

International law clearly condemns denying fundamental liberties to persons on the basis of qualities inherent to their individuality and humanity. Sexual orientation is such a quality, a deeply rooted and profoundly felt element of selfhood.[213] Article 2 of the International Covenant on Civil and Political Rights states: "Each State Party to the present Covenant undertakes to respect and to ensure to all individuals within its territory and subject to its jurisdiction the rights recognized in the present Covenant, without distinction of any kind, such as race, colour, sex, language, religion, political or other opinion, national or social origin, birth or other status." Further, Article 26 of the ICCPR states that "all persons are equal before the law and are entitled without any discrimnation to the equal protection of the law" and that "the law shall prohibit any discrimnation and guarantee to all persons equal and effective protection against discrimination on any ground such as race, colour, sex, language, religion, political or other opinion, national or social origin, property, birth or other status."

The United Nations Human Rights Committee recognizes sexual orientation as a status protected from discrimination under international law. In a 1994 decision regarding a Tasmanian law similar to Article 200, the committe unanimously held that sexual orientation is not a valid basis for discriminatory denial of rights specified in the ICCPR. The committee endorsed the plaintiff's contention that the relevant sections of the Tasmanian code "distinguish between individuals in the exercise of their right to privacy on the basis of sexual activity,

---

[213]See Human Rights Watch's policy statment on gay and lesbian rights attached as appendix II.

sexual orientation, and sexual identity."[214] In holding this to violate Article 2 of the ICCPR, the committee thus affirmed that no right recognized in the ICCPR can be recognized in varying degrees according to sexual orientation. No state may arbitrarily consign gays and lesbians to diminished and discriminatory enjoyment of any fundamental freedom.

Article 200 of the Romanian penal code on its face violates the principle articulated by the Human Rights Committee in that it punishes conduct between persons of the same sex that, when carried on between persons of opposite sexes, is either not criminal or receives a lower penalty. The law imposes a severely unequal punishment on homosexual acts "committed in public"; punishes homosexual acts committed with "minors" more severely than heterosexual acts, and sets the age of majority four years higher; and allows homosexual rape to be punished with subsequent denial of civil rights, unlike heterosexual rape. In ways both large and small, explicit and implied, Romanian law establishes the inferior status of gays and lesbians.

Despite Romanian government claims to the contrary, both the past history of the law, and its present status, reveal that the law enforces discrimination: it dictates that behaviors and expressions which identify people as gay or lesbian—whether they be sexual acts behind closed doors, or casual gestures of intimacy on the street—may render an individual subject to police harassment, abuse, and penal sanction.

The government of Romania has also contended that the new language of Article 200, paragraph 1, does not infringe on the recognized right to privacy and does not penalize private homosexual acts. However, the text of the article itself —as well as the statements of those who devised it and those who enforce it— clearly violates international norms limiting governmental interference with individuals' privacy, in that it criminalizes consensual same sex sexual relations between adults that, although carried out in private, becomes known to the public and produce "a public scandal." Article 17 of the ICCPR promises:

> 1. No one shall be subjected to arbitrary or unlawful interference with his privacy, family, home, and correspondence, nor to unlawful attacks on his honour and reputation.

---

[214] Nicholas Toonen v. Australia, U. N. GAOR, Hum. Rts. Comm., 15th Sess., Case no 488/1992, U.N. Doc. CCPR/c/50/D/488/1992. The committee declined to consider whether sexual orientation constituted an "other status" under Article 2 or Article 26 (the ICCPR's other equal-protection statement), noting simply that "the reference to 'sex' in articles 2, para. 1, and 26 is to be taken as including sexual orientation."

> 2. Everyone has the right to the protection of the law against such interference or attacks.

Similarly, Article 8 of the European Convention for the Protection of Human Rights and Fundamental Freedoms reads:

> 1. Everyone has the right to respect for his private and family life, his home and his correspondence.
> 2. There shall be no interference by a public authority with the exercise of this right except such as is in accordance with the law and is necessary in a democratic society in the interests of national security, public safety or the economic well-being of the country, for the prevention of disorder or crime, for the protection of health or morals, or for the protection of the rights and freedoms of others.

A now-substantial body of international law affirms unequivocally that laws criminalizing consensual, private sexual acts between adults are a flagrant violation of these provisions. In three successive decisions, *Dudgeon v. United Kingdom* (1981), *Norris v. Ireland* (1988), and *Modinos v. Cyprus* (1993), the European Court of Human Rights has held against sodomy laws. Although the European convention allows three qualifications upon the right to privacy—giving scope to interferences which are embodied clearly in law, serve a legitimate aim including "the protection of public morals," and are necessary to achieve that aim in a democratic society—the court has maintained that sodomy laws cannot be justified on these terms. Neither public morality nor any political exigency can override the right of lesbians, gay men, and bisexuals to sexual privacy.

In *Dudgeon*, the court held that laws penalizing such activities could not be held "necessary in a democratic society":

> Although members of the public who regard homosexuality as immoral may be shocked, offended, or disturbed by the commission by others of private homosexual acts, this cannot on its own warrant the application of penal sanctions when it is consenting adults alone who are involved.[215]

In *Norris*, the court rejected the government of Ireland's contention that "the moral fibre of a democratic nation is a matter for its own institutions," reaffirming that

---

[215] Dudgeon v. United Kingdom, 4 Eur. H. R. Rep. 149 (1981).

"such justifications as there are for retaining the law in force unamended are outweighed by the detrimental effects which the very existence of the legislative provisions can have on the life of a person of homosexual orientation."[216] Finally, in *Modinos*, the court held that even the Cypriot government's "consistent policy of not bringing criminal proceedings in respect of private homosexual conduct on the basis that the relevant law is a dead letter" was irrelevant to the government's obligation to repeal the law.[217]

Yet, although Article 200 effectively eliminates privacy protections for lesbians and gay men, the impact of so-called "sodomy laws" is still more dangerous and wide-ranging. Wherever they are in force, such laws confirm inequality throughout a roster of civil and political rights, stigmatizing homosexuals and relegating them to second-class citizenship.[218] In restricting the speech of gays and lesbians, or even speech about them, and in contravening their elemental rights to associate and assemble, Article 200 only makes particularly explicit the underlying tenor and intent of such provisions: to eliminate all visible manifestation of homosexuality, by denying gays and lesbians the equal protection of the law. That denial of equal protection in Romania is the true "public scandal."

Recommendations

Human Rights Watch and the International Gay and Lesbian Human Rights Commission therefore call on the government and parliament of Romania to eliminate legal discrimination based on sexual orientation.

1) Article 200, and any explicit mention of "sexual relations between persons of the same sex," should be eliminated from the penal code altogether. The crimes penalized in paragraphs 3 and 4 should be combined, in gender-neutral language,

---

[216] Norris v. Ireland, 13 Eur. H. R. Rep. 186 (1989).

[217] Modinos v. Cyprus: 16 Eur. H. R. Rep 485 (1993).

[218] Laws similar to Article 200 are in force in numerous jurisdictions worldwide. The exact number of so-called "sodomy laws" in existence around the globe is difficult to calculate. The very term is inaccurate: many laws, like Romania's, incriminate consensual sexual acts between women as well as "sodomy" between males. The laws may be written in widely varying ways: some regulate particular sexual acts, such as anal sex, regardless of the gender of the actors, while others specifically target same-sex sexual activities; still others may entail a blanket prohibition of "unnatural" or "indecent" acts, which may be applied with particular rigor against homosexual activity. As of 1997, the International Gay and Lesbian Human Rights Commission was aware of ninety countries which had laws fitting these descriptions in force over some or all parts of their territory.

with the relevant provisions of Article 197 on rape. Paragraph 2 should be combined with Article 198, on "sexual relations with a minor female," to create a single law criminalizing all sexual relations with minors, regardless of the gender of the actors or victims, and with a uniform penalty and age of consent. Paragraphs 1 and 5 of Article 200 should be stricken completely.

2) Other references to "public scandal" in the penal code, particularly in Article 321, should be eliminated. That law—a Communist-era provision originally punishing "hooliganism"—should be rewritten and clarified to specify the nature of deeds which "offend good morals," as should similar provisions in Law 61/1991; otherwise these laws will continue to invite discriminatory enforcement.

3) A single law should address sexual relations committed in public, whether heterosexual or homosexual, and impose a reasonable penalty, if criminalization of such relations is deemed necessary by the Romanian government. "Sexual relations" should be clearly defined in the penal code.[219] Definitions of "committed in public" and "committed in private," when applied to sexual acts, should be rendered complementarily clear, respecting personal autonomy and taking into consideration the historically problematic and vulnerable character of privacy in Romania.

4) Discrimination and interference with privacy are not features unique to Article 200: the whole corpus of laws dealing with sexuality in Romania demands revision, as a hash of overlapping and ill-defined terms. Article 201, punishing "sexual perversion," is dangerously vague and should be eliminated. Article 197 should be rewritten so that all sexual acts (clearly defined, and not restricted to vaginal intercourse) forcibly committed upon another person, without regard to gender, are explicitly criminalized and receive the same punishment. Paragraph 4 of Article 197, which exempts any rape from punishment if the victim marries even one of the assailants, should be eliminated.[220]

---

[219] Examples cited above show that this expression is subject to wildly divergent interpretations under Romanian law. There is recurrent uncertainty, for example, whether oral sex is a "sexual relation" or a "sexual perversion," or indeed whether the first of those terms subsumes the second; while the Alba Tribunal's decision on the appeal of Mariana Cetiner appears predicated on the assumption that fondling and kissing constitute a "sexual relation" between women. Only an exactitude of definition which eluded the authors of the 1936 and 1968 codes can close these latitudes and lacunae.

[220] Such laws implicitly define rape as a crime against a woman's (or a family's) honor, which can be redressed through marriage, rather than as a crime of violence against the physical integrity of the victim , which should be punished through criminal sanctions. See "A Matter of Power: State Control of Women's Virginity in Turkey," Human Rights Watch,

5) Article 309, paragraph 2 of the penal code, which specially criminalizes "transmission of AIDS" by "a person who knows him/herself to suffer from that disease," is poorly written: it ignores the actual nature and transmission of HIV[221], and does not punish *knowing* (or intended) *transmission* of "AIDS," but any transmission of the syndrome/virus by a person who knows him/herself to "have" or carry it, *regardless of intent or of any precautions which may have been taken.* It thus codifies the idea that any sexual activity on the part of people living with HIV is potentially criminal, should accepted precautions somehow fail.[222] In addition to discriminating overtly against persons living with HIV and AIDS,[223] it opens a new ground for monitoring and infringing on the rights of an already reviled group, gay men. The provision should be repealed; and the Ministry of Health should see that its own existing standards are both enforced and expanded, to protect the anonymity as well as confidentiality of HIV test results, and to ensure that no one is given an HIV test without informed consent.

June 1994.

[221] Most conspicuously, "AIDS" is not transmitted; the HIV virus is. A person who has not developed AIDS can still transmit the HIV virus to another person, who may or may not develop AIDS.

[222] The report (communicated by one policeman to Human Rights Watch and IGLHRC) that the law has already been brought to bear against a rape victim clearly shows that—in the view of those who enforce it—it may be construed to punish *inadvertent* and even *explicitly involuntary* transmission of HIV. The law seems intended not as a public-health measure but as means of controlling suspect populations, including prostitutes (against whom, according to General Paun of the IGP, the existing Article 309 was primarily enforced) and also gay men.

[223] A 1996 resolution of the United Nations Commission on Human Rights, "The protection of human rights in the context of human immunodeficiency virus (HIV) and acquired immunodeficiency syndrome (AIDS), E/CN.4/1996/43, confirms that "the term 'or other status' in non-discrimination provisions in international texts should be interpreted to cover health status, including HIV/AIDS," thus bringing HIV status under the protection of Articles 2 and 26 of the ICCPR. Resolution 1994/29 of the Sub-Commission on Prevention of Discrimination and Protection of Minorities also affirms that "discrimination on the basis of AIDS or HIV status, actual or presumed, is prohibited by existing international human rights standards and . . . the term 'other status' in non-discrimination provisions in international human rights texts should be interpreted to cover health status, including HIV/AIDS."

6) Police surveillance of gays and lesbians, including the keeping of lists, should cease; blackmail and other forms of abuse must be appropriately punished. Investigations must be launched into allegations of police brutality and torture; those responsible for such violations must be held accountable. Police and other law-enforcement officials should be trained in sensitivity to Romania's minorities, including gays and lesbians, to ensure that the formal or informal designation of minority populations as suspect classes comes to a halt.

6) Human Rights Watch and IGLHRC call for a halt to the imprisonment of persons solely for consensual sexual acts performed between adults. However, homosexuals are of course arrested and imprisoned under other charges; and any prison system is likely to contain men having sex with men, and women having sex with women, who may not identify themselves as homosexual. Such persons are frequently subjected to isolation, beatings, and other forms of abuse within the Romanian prison system. Penitentiary authorities should protect prisoners suffering from such abuse; should punish prison officials (as well as inmates) who engage in, encourage, or condone maltreatment of or discrimination against such prisoners; and should eliminate those aspects of prison governance—including the supervising-inmate system—which permit and further these abuses.

Human Rights Watch and the International Gay and Lesbian Human Rights Commission also call on international bodies to act to persuade the Romanian government to amend its laws and practices. In particular:

1) The *Council of Europe* should continue to press for full compliance on the part of the Romanian government with the commitments it undertook upon admission. The Council should make clear that this includes full repeal of both paragraph 1 and paragraph 5 of Article 200. Under Resolution 1123, passed April 24, 1997, the Parliamentary Assembly of the Council of Europe suspended for one year the procedure of reporting on Romania's progress toward fulfilling its commitments. The Council should treat this as a firm deadline for Romania to complete the remaining legal reforms specified in the resolution and in the rapporteurs' final report;[224] these explicitly include the elimination of Article 200.

The Council should also press for the repeal of other legislation which has a discriminatory impact. The Council should consider, in its future external and internal reporting procedures, recognizing gays and lesbians as a minority along with national, ethnic, and racial minorities, as this may provide a framework for

---

[224] 11 April 1997; ADOC/7795

considering questions of discrimination beyond the mere existence of "sodomy laws."[225]

2) The *Organization for Security and Cooperation in Europe*, and particularly the Office for Democratic Institutions and Human Rights, should explicitly discuss the question of discrimination against homosexuals in forums to address the implementation of commitments under the OSCE's "human dimension."[226]

3) The *European Union* should include, in its new basic treaty, specific reference to sexual orientation as a category protected against discrimination. In keeping with the principles of the 1994 Roth Report and Resolution "On equal rights for homosexuals and lesbians in the EC,"[227] discrimination against homosexuals should be explicitly investigated and taken into account as a significant aspect of the human rights records of new states applying for admission.

4) The *North Atlantic Treaty Organization* should carefully weigh the human rights records of applicant states, and particularly their treatment of minority populations, including lesbians and gays.

---

[225] Recommendation 1201 (1993) of the Parliamentary Assembly of the Council of Europe establishes principles regarding the protection of minorities. Recommendation 924 of the Parliamentary Assembly (1981) is a comprehensive statement on discrimination against homosexuals. In practice, however, rapporteurs on new states applying for admission have restricted themselves to questioning laws criminalizing private, consensual homosexual behavior between adults. The Council's reporting procedures and other forums should consider broader questions of discrimination against homosexuals in member and non-member States.

[226] The Report of Subsidiary Working Body 1 of the (then) CSCE Warsaw Human Dimension Implementation Meeting, 1993, called attention to "groups which were not 'national minorities' but which nonetheless suffered discrimination, including women, homosexuals, migrant workers, and conscientious objectors."

[227] One of the most wide-ranging statements on the rights of homosexuals made by any elected or international body thus far: European Parliament, Doc_EN/RR/244/244267.

APPENDIX I: LEGAL TEXTS

Article 200 of the penal code: 1968 version, as published in Buletinul Oficial no. 79-79/June 21,1968:

Sexual relations between persons of the same sex

1. Sexual relations between persons of the same sex are punishable by imprisonment of one to five years.
2. The acts described in paragraph 1, if committed on a minor, on a person incapable of defending him/herself or of expressing volition, or through force, are punishable by imprisonment of two to seven years.
3. If the acts described in paragraph 2 result in grave damage to bodily integrity or health, the punishment is imprisonment of three to ten years; if they result in the death or suicide of the victim, the punishment is imprisonment of seven to fifteen years.
4. Inciting or encouraging a person to practice the acts described in paragraph 1 is punishable by imprisonment of one to five years.

Article 200 of the penal code: current version, as enacted by Law 140/November 5,1996:

Sexual relations between persons of the same sex

1. Sexual relations between persons of the same sex, committed in public or if producing public scandal, are punishable by imprisonment of one to five years.
2. The act of a major having sexual relations with a minor of the same sex is punishable by imprisonment of two to seven years and denial of certain rights.
3. Sexual relations with a person of the same sex incapable of defending him/herself or of expressing volition, or through force, are punishable by imprisonment of three to ten years and denial of certain rights.
4. If the acts described in paragraphs 2-3 result in grave damage to bodily integrity or health, the punishment is imprisonment from five to fifteen years and denial of certain rights; if they result in the death or suicide of the victim, the punishment is imprisonment of fifteen to twenty-five years and denial of certain rights.
5. Inciting or encouraging a person to the practice of sexual relations between persons of the same sex, as well as propaganda or association or any other act of proselytism committed in the same scope, is punishable by imprisonment of one to five years.

Article 201 of the penal code: 1968 version, as published in Buletinul Oficial no. 79-79/June 21,1968:

Sexual perversion
1. Committing an act of sexual perversion which produces public scandal is punishable with imprisonment of one to five years.
2-4. The dispositions of Article 200, paragraphs 2-4 apply correspondingly.
An act of sexual perversion is any unnatural act in connection with sexual life, other than those described in Article 200.

Article 201 of the penal code: current version, as enacted by Law 140/November 5, 1996:

Sexual perversion
1. Acts of sexual perversion, committed in public or if producing public scandal, are punishable by imprisonment of one to five years.
2-5. The dispositions of Article 200, paragraphs 2-5 apply correspondingly.
An act of sexual perversion is any unnatural act in connection with sexual life, other than those described in Article 200.

Article 204 of the penal code, as published in Buletinul Oficial no. 79-79/June 21,1968 (unchanged in the current penal code):

Punishment of attempts
Attempts to commit the infractions described in Articles 197-198 and 200-203 are punishable.

Article 321 of the penal code, as introduced in Law 6/1973 (unchanged in the current penal code):

Outrage against good morals and disturbance of the public peace
1. The act of a person who, in public, commits deeds or gestures, proffers words or expressions, or makes any other manifestation which tends to offend good morals or to produce public scandal, is punishable by imprisonment of three months to two years, or with a fine.
2. If the acts described in paragraph 1 gravely disturb the public peace, the punishment is imprisonment of six months to five years.

Law 61/1991, as published in Monitorul Oficial no. 196/September 27, 1991 (excerpts):

A law to punish acts of violation against norms of social cohabitation, public order, and public peace

Article 1. To ensure a climate of public order and peace necessary to the normal conduct of economic and social-cultural activity, and to promote civilized relations in daily life, citizens are obliged to maintain a civil, moral and responsible demeanor, in the spirit of the laws of the country and of the norms of social cohabitation.

Article 2. The commission of any of the following acts constitutes a misdemeanor, if not performed under conditions in which, according to criminal law, they are considered criminal acts:

1. Engaging in public in obscene or injurious deeds, acts, or gestures, offensive or vulgar expressions, threats or acts of violence against persons or their reputations, which disturb the public order and peace, or which provoke the indignation of citizens or damage their dignity and honor, or that of public institutions;

2) Constituting a group formed of three or more persons, with a view to committing illicit actions, contrary to public order and peace and the norms of social cohabitation, as well as acts of encouragement or support given, in any form, to any such group of persons, which incites to social disorder; . . .

(Punishments for these offenses are detailed in a schedule of fines, which can be converted to terms of imprisonment if not paid.)

Translations by the International Gay and Lesbian Human Rights Commission

APPENDIX II: HUMAN RIGHTS WATCH POLICY ON LESBIAN AND GAY RIGHTS (1994)

Human Rights Watch opposes state-sponsored and state-tolerated violence, detention, and prosecution of individuals because of their sexual identity, sexual orientation, or private sexual practices. Human Rights Watch derives this policy from the right to life, liberty, and security of the person (Universal Declaration of Human Rights, Article 3; International Covenant on Civil and Political Rights, Articles 6 and 9), rights of freedom of expression and association (UDHR 19 and 22; ICCPR 19 and 22), the right against arbitrary detention (UDHR 9, ICCPR 9), the right to privacy (UDHR 12, ICCPR 17) and the prohibition of discrimination on the basis of status (UDHR 2, ICCPR 2, 26).

ACKNOWLEDGMENTS

This report was written by Scott Long, advocacy coordinator and european regional specialist for the International Gay and Lesbian Human Rights Commission (IGLHRC). Julie Dorf and Sydney Levy read the report for IGLHRC; Kieran Burns, Roy Dickinson, David Geer, Steffen Jensen, Kurt Krickler, Mona Nicoara, and Peter Norman all provided information and suggestions. For Human Rights Watch, the report was reviewed by Jeri Laber, Holly Cartner, Dinah PoKempner, and Cynthia Brown. Alex Frangos and Emily Shaw provided production assistance.

The report is based in part on a research mission undertaken by Human Rights Watch and IGLHRC in June and July 1997, to investigate the situation of gays and lesbians under the new law on homosexuality in Romania. Research was conducted by a working group whose members included Vera Campeanu, Daniel Iorga, Scott Long, Yves Nya Ngatchou, Mona Nicoara, and Bogdan Voicu. Members of the mission visited and interviewed inmates in fifteen penitentiaries, as well as members of parliament, representatives of the ministries of justice and the interior, and numerous local prosecutors and police. Ion Iacos and Manuela Stefanescu of the Romanian Helsinki Committee; Adrian Coman of ACCEPT; Ioana Stancel of the Asociatia Romana Anti-SIDA (ARAS); and Nicolae Stefanescu-Draganesti of the Liga Apararii Drepturilor Omului (LADO) provided invaluable assistance to the mission, as did Michael Holscher, George-Valentin Serbanescu, and Sorin Volpe. Follow-up research was also conducted by Dennis van der Veur and Adrian Coman. Human Rights Watch and IGLHRC gratefully acknowedge the cooperation of the Romanian Ministry of Justice, and especially of Ana Iacovescu, director of international relations, as well as of Col. Radu Moldovan and Col. Mircea Ruse, who together permitted unprecedentedly open access to the penitentiary system.

The report also draws on numerous fact-finding missions conducted by Scott Long, on behalf of IGLHRC and the Romanian Helsinki Committee, between 1992 and 1996. Vera Campeanu, Razvan Ion, Yves Nya Ngatchou, Mona Nicoara, Aurelian Seres, and Bogdan Voicu participated in the missions. Ion Iacos, Manuela Stefanescu, and Renate Gavrilas-Weber, of the Romanian Helsinki Committee, assisted with this work, as did, in several cases, the Societatea Independenta Romana a Drepturilor Omului (SIRDO). The first mission to investigate the situation of gays and lesbians in Romania was undertaken jointly by Russ Gage of IGLHRC, John Clark and Kurt Krickler of the International Lesbian and Gay Association, and Henning Mikkelsen of the World Health Organization in 1992. Gratitude is due them for helping to bring the issue to the attention of the human rights community; their work represents the beginning of a long campaign for change which—unfortunately—has not yet seen its final results.